The Door is Open

MEDITATIONS OF A WAYFARER

Alison Gibson

FORWARD MOVEMENT PUBLICATIONS
CINCINNATI, OHIO

The Door is Open

MEDITATIONS OF A WAYFARER

April 1978—An Easter Happening

This Easter marks the 40th anniversary of God's taking possession of my life. It was an extraordinary occurrence, the culmination of months of seeking and testing and praying.

The story begins on Labor Day 1937 when my 24-year-old brother was killed in an automobile accident on Long Island. We were only a year apart, the closest of companions and confidants. When my father called to break the tragic news, I was devastated. I needed help, strength, and comfort—not only for myself but for my parents, who had lost their only son. I sought it on my knees—the first real praying I had ever done. A peace and power not my own took possession of me and enabled me to be of some consolation to my parents during those dark days of shock and desolation.

The question of life after death was something to which I had never given any thought. Now suddenly I felt an urgent need for answers—not only concerning an afterlife but also about the meaning of this one. At every opportunity I read and studied the Bible. Above all I prayed. The more I prayed the deeper my faith became that there was, indeed, a spirit directing my life and with whom I could communicate. The message that I was getting was that God wanted me to submit my whole life to him without reservation. In my nightly prayers I seemed to be asked how serious I was in my willingness to commit myself and all I held dear to God. Questions kept recurring. "What are you ready to give up? Money and the things that money can buy? Home, family, possessions? Would I go wherever God seemed to suggest?" My answers were something like: "O, you can't be asking that, God. Well, I'll consider it but not now, maybe later."

I observed Lent that year with considerable self-discipline. Then came Holy Week and Good Friday. I entered into and observed the culminating events of Jesus' life with great intensity, so much so that when I left the three-hour Good Friday observance, I was literally unable to speak. The costliness of God's love was overwhelming.

I attended the Easter service with a heart full of joy and gratitude. The despair of Good Friday gave way to the assurance that God's power could turn defeat into victory. That night on my knees I was finally able to say "Yes" to whatever God might ask me, trusting only His love and power. At that moment, although I was in a dark room with my eyes shut, I was immersed in a brilliant light.

Simultaneously, I heard a voice clearly say: "You see Alison, it IS true, it is all true." I think for a time my breathing stopped and I entered into another world. How long I remained transfixed I do not know, but gradually the light faded and I found myself kneeling by my bed.

I have little doubt that the voice I heard all those years ago was the voice of God. Not only did the spoken words assure me that, indeed, there is life beyond the grave but, what is more, in those few moments I actually experienced it.

⚘⚘⚘

November 1, 1978—Hobe Sound, Fla.

I have been given a book by James Fenhagen entitled MORE THAN WANDERERS. I like the implication that our spiritual journey has a destination and is not just aimless wandering. I have felt this to be true despite the many detours and roadblocks which I have encountered. There has always been something within me which would not allow me to give up the search for God—which is what the journey is all about. I often wonder why some people find it easier than others to have, and to maintain, a first-hand, vital sense of God's presence. The key may be, "Except ye become as little children..." My faith has never been that simple. I want to understand with my mind as well as with my heart. God gave us our minds and surely we are meant to use them in our search for Him.

ᴎᴎᴎ

February 26, 1979

To quote from MORE THAN WANDERERS: "The Christian Journey is indissolubly linked with a person. It is not a journey we take alone. Jesus Christ is our companion. He must be as present in our lives today as He was to first century Christians."

Ash Wednesday is only two days off. I intend to make this Lent a time for seeking to know better what St. Paul meant when he wrote "Let this mind be in you which was also in Christ Jesus" (Phil. 2:5). I shall also attempt to keep a daily journal. The words journey and journal have the same derivation. Both come from the French word "jour" meaning day. One definition of journey is "a day's travel or labor." A journeyman was "one who worked by the day." A journal is an account of a day's progress on the journey.

ᴎᴎᴎ

June 21, 1979—Richmond, Va.

Today I made my greatest effort to be quiet and listen for God's voice. But I heard nothing. A picture came to mind of Peter fishing all night and catching nothing until Jesus appeared and told him to try on the other side of the boat. All of a sudden his net was filled. This story corresponds in my mind to my failed attempts to meditate. I might spend hours with nothing to reward my effort when suddenly I seem to hear Jesus telling me to try the other side. I'm not sure what "the other side" means except perhaps to try again with greater confidence, which is what I did. I was rewarded by a deeper stillness and openness to the reality of a spiritual presence.

ൟ ൟ ൟ

June 27, 1979

Thomas Kelly writes that the "Inward Christ is no mere dogma—it is the living center of reference for all Christian souls, Christian groups, yes, all non-Christian groups as well. He is the center and source of action, not the end point of thought. He is the locus of commitment, not a problem for debate."

I recognize that my whole theological focus has shifted in the past several years from propositions which I attempted to verify through experience, to an inner experience from which I draw my own propositions. I don't want to limit my faith by having it said, "This is it, this is what a professing Christian must accept."

ᛣ ᛣ ᛣ

August 4, 1979

Somewhere recently I have read, "Joy is the pennant we fly from the castle tower of our lives indicating that the King is in residence." We can experience joy in our innermost being even in the midst of grief and pain. Our hearts may ache for the suffering which exists in the world but the words of Jesus reassure us. "In this world ye shall have tribulation but be of good cheer for I have overcome the world."

ᛣ ᛣ ᛣ

September 7, 1979—Tupper Lake, NY

A perfect fall day! To be near the lake I walked down to Rocky Cove and sat down on a large flat boulder. The sun was shining intermittently as large fleecy clouds moved across the sky. All was still except for the water lapping gently at my feet. My desire was to feel myself at one with the peace and beauty of my surroundings. I tried to obliterate all conscious thought—just "let go and let God."

After sitting very quietly for some time with my eyes closed, the words of Whittier's lovely hymn came into my mind: "Breathe on me breath of God till I am wholly thine." At that moment I felt a lovely gentle breeze spring up around me and seemingly penetrate right through me.

As I recalled the next line: "till all this earthly part of me glows with a fire divine," the sun came out from behind the clouds, piercing my closed eyes with it's brilliance and enveloping me with it's warmth. I remained without moving until, minutes later, another cloud covered the sun. Then I opened my eyes and the world and I returned to normal.

ᚹᚹᚹ

December 15, 1979

A reading from MARKINGS, by Dag Hammarskjöld: "How ridiculous this need of yours to communicate. Why should it mean so much to you that at least one person has seen the inside of your life? Why should you write down all of this? For yourself, to be sure— perhaps for others as well?"

It seems a natural longing to be known intimately and accepted despite our flaws. Maybe only God can enter into the heart and soul. He created us and is aware of our innermost being. That should suffice.

ᐢᐢᐢ

December 21, 1979

A quotation on aging by Henri Nouwen: "A long life makes me feel near truth, yet it won't go into words, so how can I convey it? I can't and I want to. I want to tell people approaching and perhaps fearing age that it is a time of discovery. If they ask 'of what?' I can only answer 'We must each find out for ourselves, otherwise it won't be discovery.'"

ᐢᐢᐢ

January 26, 1980

Another quote on the subject of aging: "If we are old and uninteresting, it is so to the world which is passing away moment by moment. To God, who made each of us for Himself, we are not uninteresting. And what we are to Him, that is what we really are. If our life is hid with Christ in God, however silently the years pass, we shall grow in humility in that secret place; our stillness will be full of happiness because it is filled with love."

Dear God, in stillness may I grow in humility and be filled with happiness, which is the fruit of love. Amen.

ᛝᛝᛝ

March 2, 1980—Hobe Sound, Fla.

I'm sitting on the patio under a bright blue sky, the temperature is in the 80's, a small bird is chirping, and there are flowers in abundance wherever I look. Some would call it paradise. Certainly, all the ingredients are here—beauty, security, pleasure, physical fitness, friendship, and a lot more. But, for me, something is missing. I feel an unprofitable servant. There's so little opportunity to serve, isolated as we are here from the world's suffering. I am not involved in any worthwhile cause. Perhaps the challenge of life is over for me. Will I ever again have the opportunity to serve—and do I really want to? Am I still ready to take risks and surrender the ease and security which I now possess?

I believe that if there is something God would have me do or somewhere He'd have me go He would make it clear to me! But perhaps I'm not listening or perhaps I'm not ready (even at age 69) to obey. So this Lent should be a time to listen.

❦❦❦

May 7, 1980

St. Paul writes to the Corinthians, "The Spirit explores everything, even the depth of God's own nature."

Being an explorer myself I was delighted to come upon these words. They encourage me to continue my search for a concept of God that will satisfy both my intellect and my soul. It seems to me that we must spend our lives searching for meaning and attempting to articulate what we believe in our hearts.

❦❦❦

May 8, 1980

According to Matthew's Gospel, Jesus told His disciples: "Ask, and it will be given you; search, and you will find; knock and the door will be opened for you."

I heard in a sermon that these are ongoing verbs, describing continuous action. You don't just ask and stop asking, knock once and give up or ever stop seeking. I think I am destined to go on searching the rest of my days, at least until God makes Himself known to me.

ℵℵℵ

June 27, 1980

In Elizabeth O'Connor's EIGHTH DAY OF CREATION I came across this: "To answer the question 'What does the Lord require of you?' I would suggest that what the Lord requires of you is that you should knock yourself out your whole life long to find what is required of you."

I often think of my life as a quest because for me questioning is so much a part of my search for God—and of my nature!

ℵℵℵ

June 30, 1980

When St. Francis de Sales was asked by a disciple: "Sir, you speak so much of the love of God, but you never tell us how to achieve it. Won't you tell me how one comes to love God?" St. Francis replied: "There is only one way and that is to LOVE him." "But you don't understand my question. What I asked was HOW do you engender this love of God?" And St. Francis said:

"By loving Him." Once again the disciple came with the same question: "But what steps do you take? Just what must I do to come into possession of this love?" St. Francis replied "You begin loving and go on loving, and loving teaches you how to love. And the more you love, the more you learn to love."

ᛈᛈᛈ

July 10, 1980

From MARKINGS: "Goodness is something so simple: always live for others, never to seek one's own advantage."

These days the tragic plight of the "Boat People," refugees from Vietnam and Cambodia, is in the forefront of the news. How heartrending that these poor people, through no fault of their own, must suffer so. My heart is moved by their condition and yet how little, if at all, my life is touched by their tragedy. I pray for them and contribute small amounts to relief organizations. I thank God for the courage and commitment of relief workers. Is there more that I can do?

Quakers believe in two dimensions of concern: the first one is an all embracing, caring love for all mankind, and the other is a particular, individual

God-given concern for the people and causes closest to us. "We cannot die on every cross, nor are we expected to." That's reassuring but does not give us leave to ignore the distant need for the more pressing ones at hand.

ᛣᛣᛣ

August 2, 1980—Tupper Lake

How wonderful (I really mean full of wonder) to be back. I so love this place! It's filled with memories of happy times—of good friends and of family gatherings. I never cease to marvel at the natural beauty—the woods, the lake, and the ever-changing sky. My heart sings out, "The heavens declare the glory of God and the firmament showeth forth his handiwork."

It is hard for me to reconcile the contrast between the peace and the beauty of this place with the suffering and violence that afflicts so much of the world. Not only are there the man-made agonies of war, persecution and injustice, but there are natural disasters like earthquakes, drought, and famine. The former are more easily understood (if not accepted) as the result of evil. The latter are harder to understand. While we in the Western Hemisphere enjoy *prosperity, many people live in areas of the earth which are bleak and barren.*

At the present time the inhabitants of Northern Uganda are starving. They have no rain—the crops are withering and animals are dying due to a lack of water.

Why this inequality? Surely those of us in the western world are no more deserving of the earth's bounty than those who live in Africa, India, Bangladesh, North Korea. How do these poor, deprived people conceive of a just and loving God? Questions like these have perplexed the minds of men and troubled their hearts from the earliest of times. The Old Testament prophets and authors of the psalms continually beseeched God to spare his people. Their cry is still on the lips of modern man: "How long, O Lord, How long?" The question remains unanswered.

ᴘᴘᴘ

November 1, 1980

"Blessed are the poor in spirit." To be blessed (the French word is blessé, wounded) means to be open and vulnerable. It strikes me that all the Beatitudes contain this idea of openness and defenselessness. Only so can we be filled.

Jesus' ministry was always open to the needs of others and He was ready to bear the burdens of the poor, the lost, and the bereaved. He calls us to do the same. Compassion is not a safe emotion. It involves a willingness to share suffering, but in so doing we shall be called "Children of God and partakers of His kingdom."

℘℘℘

November 11, 1980

There's a current TV show called "One Day at A Time." That is the way I'm trying to live my life. "Be not anxious for the morrow." Today in FORWARD DAY BY DAY one sentence jumped out at me: "God hasn't finished with you yet." We are all incomplete—a "work in progress." What a heartening thought that is when confronted with our many faults and failures. Each day gives us another chance to become what God would have us to be. In his epistle to the Philippians, St. Paul writes: "I am sure that He who began a good work in you will bring it to completion at the day of Jesus Christ."

℘℘℘

November 13, 1980

God's spirit within is constantly compelling us to become the person He wants us to be. The unforgivable sin is the sin against the Holy Spirit—the refusal to follow where He leads. According to John Coburn (CHRIST'S LIFE: OUR LIFE) the only final sin is to give up. No matter how often we stumble, He puts us back on our feet and says: "Try again." We cannot grow spiritually except through temptation and failure.

☙☙☙

November 16, 1980

In his journal PRAY TO LIVE, Thomas Merton writes: "My God, I have no idea where I'm going. I do not see the road ahead of me, I cannot know for certain where it will end. Nor do I really know myself, and the fact that I think I am following your will does not mean I am actually doing so. But I believe that the desire to please you does, in fact, please you and I hope I have that desire in all that I am doing. I hope that I will never do anything apart from that desire. And I know that if I do this you will lead me by the right road, though I may know nothing about it. Therefore I will trust you always though I may seem to be lost. For you are ever with me and you will never leave me to face my perils alone."

How surprising, but how encouraging to know that a man of such spiritual stature as Merton only vaguely senses what is God's destiny for him. I remember reading somewhere that obedience is the precursor of faith. Only as we obey will the next step in the journey be shown to us. The important thing is to say "yes" and trust the Spirit's guidance.

ﾉﾟﾉﾟﾉﾟ

November 20, 1980

A voluntary 24-hour fast is being observed by the downtown churches. It is scheduled to end at 6:30 this evening with a joint worship service. I am observing the fast but can't attend the service as we are having guests for dinner. This takes some of the incentive away, as the fast becomes personal rather than corporate.

It is, however, in the larger sense corporate as it is a means of identifying with hungry people the world over. Those gnawing pangs in one's stomach are a reminder of what millions of people feel daily. The fact that I've fasted for 24 hours in no way alleviates their suffering but it does, in some mysterious way, bind me to them.

"Blessed are the hungry," or, according to Luke, "Blessed are those who hunger for righteousness." My hunger for food is only temporary and self-imposed. I know that I shall soon eat. My hunger for righteousness is real enough, but can't compare with that all consuming, single-minded craving that the hungry person has for food. With such a person nothing else matters but to be filled. This is how we who have food should hunger for righteousness and justice. I've often wondered why Luke and Matthew have such different versions of the Beatitudes and which of the two might have been the words of Jesus. Now it is apparent to me how one version sheds light on the other and so both can be considered 'authentic.' Luke (or was it Jesus?) saw the relationship between hungering for food and hungering for righteousness 2000 years ago. I have only just perceived it.

℘℘℘

December 8, 1980

Today's FORWARD DAY BY DAY contains a quotation from Bonhoeffer: "One waits and hopes and putters about, but the door is shut and can only be opened from the outside. My life in a prison cell reminds me of Advent, listening for the sound of a key that will swing wide the door for a finer, freer human existence."

I think that when the door is opened we are freed from the prison cell of self-interest and given the opportunity to use our newfound freedom in the service of others.

So many innocent people are in prison today because of their faith. With what patient hope they must listen for the sound of that key. For some it will never come. Amnesty International is an organization that does provide a glimmer of hope for those forgotten men and women who are imprisoned and often tortured because they have stood for justice and truth.

"O God be with all prisoners and captives, especially the hostages in Iran. Ease their suffering and keep alive their hope. Bless and prosper the endeavors of those who are working for their release." Amen.

ᛣᛣᛣ

January 5, 1981

Some impulse made me pull from my bookcase Evelyn Underhill's FRUITS OF THE SPIRIT, which I hadn't read for 25 years. It deals with St. Paul's list of spiritual gifts as set forth in Gal 5:22. The list begins with love and ends with meekness and temperance (also defined as humility and self-control). These last two fruits are what Evelyn Underhill calls the "graces of the self-forgetful soul." They are the last and hardest spiritual traits to be acquired. For a long time we do not even see the need for them. We know that love is the essence of the Christian life. Joy and peace are what we crave for ourselves and for others. We recognize the need for suffering and gentleness if we are to follow the example of Jesus. Without goodness and faithfulness our discipleship would be ineffectual. We want to be "doers of the word, not hearers only." But without meekfulness and self-control we tend to follow our own agenda and our own gratification. Evelyn Underhill tells a story of an Anchoress, a great spiritual confessor and counselor to whom many travelers went to for advice. When the road is moved and the Anchorhold is left isolated from the busy world, her gifts no longer seem needed. Instead of becoming frustrated and hurt, the Anchoress accepts her new circumstances and sets about mending the toys the village children bring her. The manner in which she accepts the change is, according to Evelyn Underhill, "the crowning grace to her inner life."

Would that we all could accept disappointment with such grace and find new ways of exercising our faith. A prayer in FORWARD DAY BY DAY: "Lord, in the small part of your creation for which I am responsible, let me use faithfully the tools of mind and heart you have provided." Amen.

৵৵৵

January 25, 1981

In yesterday's Gospel we read: "They begged Jesus to leave the district" and today—still in Matthew— we read, "They left their nets and followed him."

It's probably just coincidence that both passages use the word "leave," but with quite different meanings. In the first story the intention is to put distance between Jesus and the local citizens because he was seen as a threat to their lifestyle. The second story is the exact opposite: the disciples gladly give up their former lifestyle in order to follow Jesus.

Jesus, still today, challenges our lifestyle and disturbs our complacency. How much are we willing to change the way we live in order to follow Him?

৵৵৵

April 14, 1981

I like St. John's version of "the anointing at Bethany" better than those in the Synoptics. He makes the setting more intimate—Jesus is being honored at dinner to which his closest friends, Lazarus, Martha and Mary, as well as his twelve disciples, have been invited. Martha was helping to wait on the table and it was Mary who poured precious ointment on Jesus' feet. And Judas was the one who protested such extravagance. Perhaps John was simply portraying the people mentioned in characteristic roles.

Mark describes the dinner as having taken place at the house of Simon "the Leper," also in Bethany. But no names are given to the other guests. Indeed, the woman in Mark is said to have come from the street and those who protest her action remain unidentified.

I like to think that Jesus, during that last ominous, hectic week, could spend some time among friends who loved and cared for him. It was an occasion they would never forget.

ﻌ ﻌ ﻌ

July 10, 1981

Someone has suggested a working creed: "There is a God. He has a will. Find it. Follow it. Then relax! Don't try so much, trust more. Let God do it for you, through you. He will." St. Paul writes, "I can do all things through Christ who strengthens me."

I have come to the end of this journal and I shall not even try to keep one while we are on vacation. When I return home I hope I can record that I was able to relax and let God's grace flow through me in such a way that it touched the lives of all who came to visit us.

ҌҌҌ

October 26, 1981

Psalm 119 as interpreted in PSALMS NOW: "O God I want so very much to please you, To walk in your ways and to carry out Your purposes; There is nothing as important to me as being in the center of your will and living within your design for my life."

I think I really mean this insofar as I can measure my own desires. However I'm sure there are hidden areas of resistance deep within my heart. What about my vanity, my desire for recognition, appreciation, and reward? I'm generous on occasion but I want my gifts acknowledged. I am not able to "give and not to count the cost." I am prone to keep a mental record of who owes me what.

I know these faults of mine are not pleasing to God and are impediments to my carrying out His purpose for my life. I am not alone, however. The psalmist asks in the 4th verse: "How can I live a life that is pleasing to you, O Lord? My instincts are earthbound. The ephemeral delights of this life tantalize and tempt me. My insatiable longings and desperate attempts to please you are thwarted by the innumerable enemies of my soul. I fail so often to do what I really want to do, to attain what I strive for, and I fall back in shame and am flattened in despair. You do forgive me when I fail, O Lord, you put me upon my feet again. You have promised to strengthen me and to sustain me in my daily conflicts. Now I pray for the wisdom to discern your will and the grace to carry it out."

I must learn to trust more in God's forgiveness and not in my own abilities. I should not be concerned about failing in what I undertake. The psalm continues: "How I praise you, O Lord, because you love me even when I fail—You continue to hold me within your loving embrace." And finally: "Now bless and guide me and give me the grace to walk within your will and purpose and have the joy of knowing that I am pleasing you." Amen.

ᛣᛣᛣ

April 5, 1982

Yesterday was Palm Sunday. The message that seems to underlie this day's celebration is humility. Jesus' choice of an ass instead of a horse is symbolic of the role he chose for himself. Although He was being hailed as a king, He perceived His vocation as that of a servant.

The collect for Palm Sunday says that Jesus in his willingness to "take our nature and to suffer death upon the cross" (as well as all the other indignities) has given us an example of his great humility which we are called to follow.

ᛣᛣᛣ

April 6, 1982

Today's gospel focuses on Jesus' authority, which was often evident in what he said and did. He denounced the hypocrisy of the ruling class, he defied their laws, and he drove corrupt merchants from the temple.

How do humility and authority exist in the same person? I think the answer is that the truly humble person does not act on his own. He is, rather, submissive to the power of God which works through him. He takes no credit for his actions. His authority comes from God.

⟡⟡⟡

April 8, 1982

Maundy Thursday. In the story of Jesus washing his disciples' feet, we see how humility and authority combine in the same act. It was a very menial and humbling task to wash another's feet but when Peter rebuked Jesus, saying, "You, Lord, washing my feet?" Jesus responded, "Do you understand what I have done for you? You call me Master and Lord, and rightly so, for that is what I am." In so saying he asserts his authority but he goes on to explain that 'Lordship' must mean servanthood and he tells his disciples to follow his example.

How often do we feel that some act is beneath us; that our status is threatened and we will be seen as inferior? In the same vein we seek recognition and appreciation for what we do. We fail to understand that what we do is by God's grace.

James and John demanded front row seats in heaven next to Jesus. They thought they had earned this privilege but were quickly rebuked when Jesus asked if they were prepared to "drink the cup that I drink or be baptized with the water I'm baptized with?" They wanted to have status and authority, but they hadn't learned the lesson of humility and service to others.

℘℘℘

April 9, 1982

Good Friday. Today, in John's Gospel, we read of Jesus' prediction that Peter will deny him three times, which Peter then does. Realizing what he'd done only after Jesus looked at him, Peter must have been overcome with guilt and remorse. But Jesus had compassion for him and offered him the opportunity to make up for his cowardice. Before their final parting Jesus asks him three times, "Simon, son of John, do you love me more than all else?" Each time Peter affirms his love, to which Jesus replies, "Feed my sheep."

It is reassuring to realize that we, like Peter, are given a second chance. In one way or another we all deny Jesus as our Lord in the ordinary events of our daily lives. It is to be hoped that we can respond as Peter did when offered forgiveness and another chance. Jesus does not want us to be undone by feelings of guilt. Rather he would have us make amends by a life of service to others.

ΚΟΚΟΚΟ

April 10, 1982

The only way that we can be sure that Jesus is our Lord is by experiencing his presence. This seems to me to be the point of Luke's story about the disciples who encountered Jesus on the road to Emmaus. At first they did not recognize him. Evidently his appearance differed from that of the man they had known so well before his death. Whether he took the form of a flesh and blood man who really walked and talked with them is a matter of conjecture, but there was definitely a presence that communicated with them as they considered the events of the past few days. It was not until the blessing of the bread that "their eyes were opened and they recognized Him." At that moment the physical person (whatever form it was) disappeared, but the disciples had no doubt that it had been Jesus who had been with them. This was because "their hearts were on fire when he talked with them."

Our hearts, then, are more to be trusted than our minds. It is within the deepest recesses of our being that we discover with certainty that Jesus is our very present Lord. I believe that every individual must make this discovery for themselves. The resurrection appearance confirmed for the disciples that Jesus was indeed Lord. It can do the same for us.

ΚΟΚΟΚΟ

April 11, 1982—Easter

I have in mind a wonderful old mission hymn that goes: "He lives, He lives, Christ Jesus lives today! You ask me how I know He lives—He lives within my heart!"

This is the greatest assurance of the resurrected Christ that we can ever have.

ΚΟΚΟΚΟ

November 1, 1982—All Saints' Day

"For in the multitude of your saints you have surrounded us with a great cloud of intercessors, that we may rejoice in their fellowship and run with endurance the race that is set before us."

I never cease to be thankful to God for all the "saints," men and women, who have inspired, instructed and encouraged me on my spiritual journey. It goes without saying that Jesus, who said, "I am the Way, the Truth, and the Life," heads the list. I would put St. Paul next because he is so honest in wrestling with his own problems. To bring my list up to date I would include Bonhoeffer, Evelyn Underhill, Archbishop Temple, Dag Hammarskjöld, Thomas Kelly, Henri Nouwen, and more recently, Frederick Buechner. Of course, there are many more.

I include Buechner because of having just read THE SACRED JOURNEY, the story of his life up to the time he entered seminary. He claims that we all have "sacred journeys" in which, if we look back, we can discern God's hand drawing us even closer to Him. Incidents to which we attached no particular significance at the time can, with hindsight, be seen as an act of God. If we had eyes to see, every moment of our days (even the boring ones) would have meaning and therefore would be sacred.

This is the way I would like to live my life—seeing God in every encounter and in all circumstances.

Dear God, I rejoice in the fellowship of all your saints who have helped me "to run the race" which you have set before me. Amen.

ᵔᵔᵔ

November 3, 1982

In Jacques Ellul's PRAYER AND THE MODERN MAN, *he speaks of prayer as being combat. A strange notion at first but, reading over old journals (dating back to the 50's) I realize how much wrestling I have done in the process of spiritual growth. Often I have been tempted to abandon the effort as futile and fruitless. Indeed there were years when I did so. But there was always within me that which kept drawing me back to what I once experienced (this refers to an Easter happening back in 1938) and forward to an unknown goal.*

Ellul asks: "Must we say that it is first of all a combat against self? The time of abandonment is something we live and feel within ourselves. The Christian has found doubt, discord, and loss of the joyful certainties, so we have to struggle to conquer and convince ourselves. Each time we undertake to pray it is a victory over temptation, over the giving up of the struggle with self, over the 'divided heart.'"

I am sure perseverance, often amid doubts and when God seems absent, is what we must practice. "Oh God, who has called us to your service, show us the purpose of our lives; though it be hard, make us long to follow it and give us courage to persevere till, at last, we reach the goal which you have set for us. Through Jesus Christ. Amen."

I don't know the source of this prayer, but it corresponds exactly to my need at the moment.

ϰϰϰ

November 14, 1982

Hebrews 10:31. "It is a fearful thing to fall into the hands of the living God."

There are times when we encounter God as terrible, remote and unknowable. There are times when God is known only by His absence. At such times we know pain, fear, depression, hurt and loneliness.

It is in the acceptance of these trials that we entrust ourselves wholly to the unseen God. Trusting that His (apparent) absence is a necessary discipline for our spiritual growth.

ϰϰϰ

January 10, 1983

In *Elizabeth O'Connor's* JOURNEY INWARD, JOURNEY OUTWARD *she writes: "Most of our days are not filled with events that we label* IMPORTANT. *The content and quality of our lives is determined by how we respond to the ordinary, and that depends on whether or not we take time to nourish our inner life."*

We must be able to recognize opportunities when they present themselves. Jesus' ministry consisted of always being ready, no matter how busy, or how tired he was, to respond when anyone came to Him with a need. Often his disciples tried to protect Him, but He was not deterred. The essential point is that Jesus' response was immediate and automatic. He didn't think twice about helping someone, nor did He weigh their merits. It was, I believe, the time Jesus spent in prayer that prepared Him to put other people's needs before His own.

For my part, I am kind, considerate and generous when it suits me and when I consider the appeal reasonable. It is not second nature with me to give unquestioningly of myself. I will only become so as I identify more clearly with Jesus, see people as He does, and serve them in His name.

℘℘℘

February 7, 1983

St. Paul's (Richmond) "Walk-In Ministry" has been, and will continue to be, a marvelous learning experience. It reveals my faults and failures, but it also provides fresh opportunity each Thursday to do a better job—i.e. to put into practice what I've learned the prior week. I see not only where I have failed but also where I've grown. To listen with empathy is, I think, the greatest contribution I can make. It's hard to listen patiently to problems beyond my ability to solve. I am a practical person and I am frustrated when I can't find a practical solution.

~ ~ ~

April 20, 1983

I think I tend to overstress the obligations of being a Christian, rather than the joy. Nearly everyone at the conference I've just attended expressed thankfulness for God's gifts to them. It makes me stop and wonder if there is something lacking in my own response. Am I sufficiently thankful for all that God has done for me? Or is my discipleship at times a burden? I'm always conscious of what should be done—by me, by other people, by the parish. Whatever we do to promote God's Kingdom should be inspired by gratitude, not obligation.

ഗ്ഗ്ഗ്

May 1983—Pentecost

How great and glorious a thing it is to celebrate the coming of the Holy Spirit. What would our lives—my life—be without God's Spirit to guide and support us?

It is through the gift of the Spirit that my life has found direction, courage, hope. Love is a gift of the Spirit, so too is the promise of eternal life—that abundant life here and now which is a foretaste of the Life to come. St. John wrote that "When He comes who is the Spirit of truth, He will guide you into all truth."

Dear God, I thank you for the gifts of the Spirit. May they continue to grow in me. Amen.

ഗ്ഗ്ഗ്

July 23, 1983

Back at Tupper Lake alone with Bob. These past few days have been as beautiful as any I can remember.

We arrived late Tuesday P.M., a hot day with the temperature reaching almost 90 degrees. The lake was shimmering in the heat, pale blue and silver, not a ripple stirring the water. The surface looked as if it had been sprayed with enamel, it was so smooth and shiny. Wednesday was a gray day—the sky filled with heavy dark clouds and the lake resembled pewter. All afternoon thunderstorms brought respite from the heat, as well as cool fresh air from the north. Thursday was a perfect Adirondack day—a stiff breeze, a cloudless sky reflected in the deep blue of the lake. Yesterday yet another transformation took place. The sun was bright but unlike yesterday, the sky was filled with fleecy white clouds. After supper we took the canoe out in time to watch the sun disappear behind Mt. Arab. As we watched, a nearly full moon rose over the tops of the clouds and sailed free in a pale twilight sky. Like a giant pumpkin a face seemed to have been carved on its surface. Meanwhile the western horizon became streaked with orange, and in the aftermath of the setting sun, the eastern sky was a tumult of gray and rosy clouds. As we paddled back to the dock the colors slowly faded and the lake reflected the black shadows of the surrounding trees.

The moon rose higher and we waited for the first stars to appear.

How blessed we are to have this beautiful place to which we can return each year. It is an unending source of renewal and recreation.

❧❧❧

August 2, 1983

This is our last day alone. Tomorrow members of the family begin to arrive. We will have a full house—nine in all—and I shall have my hands full planning and preparing meals. I am all too aware of my tendency to get uptight, impatient, and even resentful when I think I'm overburdened.

"Please God, help me to find joy in serving those I love and forget about wanting to feel that my efforts are appreciated." Amen.

❧❧❧

September 3, 1983

O Lord, I have failed you again. I lost my temper with two of my daughter's friends who overstayed their welcome.

Will I ever learn? Now that they have gone I'm

filled with remorse. I was too concerned with myself and not about the pleasure of our guests. This happened despite my prayers and good resolutions.

᠊᠊᠊ᛣᛣᛣ᠊᠊᠊

December 12, 1983

On my 72nd birthday I want to recollect the many blessings of my life.

First I am thankful for 48 years of a wonderfully happy marriage and a husband who loves and cares for me despite my faults. Our marriage might have foundered and broken like so many others had it not been undergirded by our shared faith in God and the gifts of His Spirit—forgiveness, gentleness, understanding.

All my life I've been blessed with excellent health, with an active intellect and with an appreciation of all things beautiful—for these I am thankful.

I have a lovely, spacious home set in tranquil surroundings and we have our beloved camp in the Adirondacks where children and grandchildren come to visit. For both these places I give thanks.

St. Paul's, my church home, is a source of inspiration, fellowship and growth. I have had opportunities to serve on the Vestry and to direct our Walk-In Ministries. For these and every call to serve and witness I am grateful.

Dear Lord, as my years increase, so, too, may my faith.

𝒦𝒦𝒦

December 30, 1983

"Heavenly Father, whose blessed Son came not to be served but to serve, bless all who, following in His steps, give themselves to the service of others; that with wisdom, patience, and courage they may minister in His name to the suffering, the friendless, and the needy."

In my opinion the greatest Christians in the world today are those dedicated men and women who commit themselves to confronting injustice, feeding the hungry, housing the homeless and aiding the destitute. I am thinking not only of those here in this country who run soup kitchens, homeless shelters, and minister to prisoners, but others who have gone to remote countries to serve refugees, relieve the victims of floods and earthquakes and to preach the gospel. Their lives must be lonely, frustrating and dangerous. They need our support and our prayers.

𝒦𝒦𝒦

January 20, 1984

I came across this prayer in FORWARD DAY BY DAY: "Our Father, I thank You for such strength of body, intelligence of mind, kindness of heart, and love for you as You have given me. I pray that the gifts which are within may not be lost through disuse, but developed through good use for greater service to the world and to Your kingdom."

To encounter Jesus is to let Him help us find within ourselves the faith and courage to meet all life's adventures. He would not want us to use Him as a crutch, but to stand confidently on our own two feet, using the gifts He has bestowed upon us. This is what He did for others and this is what He will do for us.

※ ※ ※

October 12, 1984

Yesterday, while I was praying I thought I heard a voice from within saying: "Be patient with the faults of others as I am patient with yours." God's patience is infinite and his forgiveness has no limits. How many times have I failed to live up to my faith or broken my resolutions? I can say most sincerely the words of St. Paul: "The good that I would I do not; the evil that I would not, that I do." God, in his mercy, does not give up on me. When I fall He lifts me up and gives me another chance. O Lord, I am grateful.

ᴷᴾᴷᴾᴷᴾ

October 16, 1984

"Oh God, help me so that all I do today I may do with serenity, without haste and without anxiety."

This prayer is prompted because of a very busy week ahead—more entertaining than I can easily manage. I know how prone I am to get nervous and overwrought by many responsibilities. I am so anxious for things to go right. I suspect the reason I find it hard to relax and enjoy is that my own self-image is involved. I want to see myself as a successful hostess.

I am reminded of Jesus' words to Martha: "Martha, you are fretting and fussing about so many things." There is a tension between the Martha and Mary sides of my personality. I want so much to have the Mary side predominate, but more often it is Martha who insists on having all in order.

ᴷᴾᴷᴾᴷᴾ

October 17, 1984

Bob woke this morning with nausea and severe pains in his chest. After calling the doctor I drove him to the hospital where he had a cardiogram. The doctor thought it best that he be put in intensive care even though the chance of a heart attack was only one in a hundred. Given Bob's excellent health and no family history of heart disorder, I found no cause for alarm and indeed he was released the next day.

But the very experience of rushing him to the hospital and the uncertainty of the outcome made me ponder many things. First, how prone we are to take our loved ones for granted. We assume that their love and companionship will continue indefinitely. We can scarcely imagine our lives without them. I have been made to think of the many wives who rush their husbands to the hospital, never to bring them home. Life is much more precious than we realize. I tend to be an optimist, assuming everything will turn out o.k. I would like to think this is because my trust is in God's providence.

Today's FORWARD DAY BY DAY seemed to address this very subject: "The Christian will, in all likelihood, be given hope. This hope will not be just a more optimistic reading of external circumstances. It will be the confidence in the creative working of God in and through the worst, for the opening of new possibilities. The angels or messengers of God give heart to the saying: 'Have no fear; keep up your courage.' This comes not from confidence in self but in the living, working God."

I pray that if I ever have to face the worst I shall have this confidence.

ॐ ॐ ॐ

December 15, 1984

Last Wednesday was my 73rd birthday and it was a lovely day! What a lot I have for which to give thanks! I am especially conscious of the blessing of good health since I have so many friends and acquaintances who are ailing in mind or in body. I would hate to think I had come to the end of my usefulness and might become a burden to others. It is so great to wake up each day with a sense of well being and purpose. I know that this will not always be the case—I shall grow old and decrepit, but as long as health and energy are granted to me, I shall rejoice and be glad and seek to use all my faculties.

I just found the following prayer tucked in my mother's Bible. It is from St. Teresa of Avila. "Let nothing disturb you, nothing frighten you. All things are passing. God never changes. Patience obtains all things. Nothing is wanting to him who possesses God. God alone suffices."

₭₭₭

December 16, 1984

Today's FORWARD DAY BY DAY's *message is about waiting. It points out that Jesus, in the last week of his life, relinquished control of events and waited for the inevitable outcome. There is a transition in Jesus' ministry from active to passive, from being a 'doer' to being 'done to.'*

A book by the English theologian W.H. Vanstone entitled THE STATUE OF WAITING *is quoted as saying that the "act of waiting can be the most intense and poignant of all human experiences." It goes on to say that the experience is one which "strips us of affectation and self-deception and reveals to us the reality of our needs, our values, and ourselves."*

I must get this book. It certainly challenges our conventional ideas about being "doers of the word."

₭₭₭

December 18, 1984

Today's meditation points to the contrast between Isaiah's prophecy of the coming Messiah: "For unto you a child is born and dominion is laid upon His shoulders. He shall be called Wonderful, Mighty God, Prince of Peace;" with the final events of Jesus' life: He was tried before the Sanhedrin, accused of blasphemy, mocked by soldiers and challenged to say if He were the Christ. To all this Jesus remained silent.

When we celebrate the birth of Christ, our Savior, we should also remember the cost of salvation. I remember one long ago Christmas when I was on my knees giving thanks for the birth of the Christ Child. The choir had begun to proceed up the aisle when, still on my knees, the cross passed by. Here was a reminder that the life which began that first Christmas ended on Good Friday in apparent defeat and disaster. Jesus let men do to Him as they wished but theirs was not the final verdict.

ℵℵℵ

December 23, 1984

This Christmas season so very many of God's children have no reason to rejoice. In Ethiopia they are dying of hunger; in India thousands are victims of a chemical explosion; women all over the world suffer imprisonment and even torture; here in the U.S. multitudes are jobless and homeless.

How can we make merry this Christmas in the face of so much pain? Christ came into the world to bring abundant life to all, but, sadly, those of us who are called to be channels of that life are too preoccupied with our own need to take much notice of the truly needy. We make the excuse that there is nothing we can do and so we absolve ourselves of responsibility and turn our backs. God, however, feels the world's pain, and if we are serious about our Christian commitment, we must be willing to do so, too.

Dietrich Bonhoeffer, who spent more than one Christmas in prison during the horrors of Nazi Germany, wrote to a friend: "It is not some religious act which makes a Christian what he is but the participation in the suffering of God in the life of the world."

ΚΡΚΡΚΡ.

December 31, 1984

Today marks the end to 1984. Tomorrow a New Year begins. My hope is that it will be a happier, more peaceful, less violent, and more just world than the one drawing to a close.

The start of a New Year is like the birth of a baby—so young, so innocent, and so full of hope and promise, so vulnerable to pain and disillusionment. In each one of us there is the potential of a new birth—the emergence from within of God's Spirit with all it's susceptibility to joy and sorrow, hope and despair, growth and discovery.

For myself I pray for greater responsibility to the needs of others. It's all very well to be concerned for the world's suffering people but I must not ignore the needs of those closest to me. For those far off all I can do is pray and make contributions to relief organizations. For those with whom I have direct contact—family, friends and neighbors—I can offer sympathy, understanding, and love. I can also refrain from being critical and judgmental. I have so many blessings and so much cause to be thankful.

I have just finished reading in FORWARD DAY BY DAY that "Thanksgiving is self-forgetful. When we forget ourselves—the image we try to project, the turf we try to defend—we make our true gift of self, the Christ within available and accessible."

Today's FORWARD DAY BY DAY reading ends a three-month section written by an anonymous woman whom I feel I've come to know and love. Her meditations have been very meaningful to me—so many shared insights, along with some new ones, that I feel extremely grateful.

ᴘᴘᴘ

January 19, 1985

Ephesians 4:2. "Be humble always and gentle, and patient too. Be forbearing with one another and charitable."

These words seem to be addressed to me. I'm neither forbearing nor charitable in many of my personal relationships. I must keep reminding myself that different as we are, we are all God's beloved children made in His image. We are also unique and endowed with our own particular gifts. This should be a cause for thanks. It would be a pretty dull world if we were all alike. It is the gift of God's Spirit that makes it possible to transcend, instead of deplore, our differences.

To the Philippians, Paul wrote: "Let your bearing towards one another arise out of your life in Christ Jesus." In the King James Version, it says "Let this mind be in you which was also in Christ Jesus." Can we ever have the mind of Christ? This is an awesome idea indeed. It is only attainable through much prayer. When, however, we come close to having His mind we will see all people as He does.

ᑭᑭᑭ

February 23, 1985

Another "Quiet Day." I love these oases in my life where I can become immersed in a spiritual ambience with a few other "fellow travelers." Most important is the realization that the Lord is in our midst.

I have chosen two books for Lenten reading: John Coburn's CHRIST'S LIFE—OUR LIFE and a book entitled MERTON'S PALACE OF NOWHERE—A SEARCH FOR GOD THROUGH AWARENESS OF THE TRUE SELF. The two together may help me reconcile different concepts of God which have long confused me. I like to address God as "Abba, Father," which for me denotes a loving relationship with a God who is other than myself. But I also think of God as "[He] in whom I live and move and have my being." Recently I've come across quite another concept—My "Me" is God. That will take a lot of reflection.

Today's FORWARD DAY BY DAY has this prayer: "O Lord, I surrender my worried way to thee and ask for faith enough to follow thy will and for the strength and relaxation to do it." I need this prayer. I need to stop reaching for answers and let God reveal Himself to me.

As for a concept of self, I conjure up the image of a caterpillar shedding its old skin to let the butterfly emerge from within. The "true self" of which both Coburn and Merton speak breaks out from the encumbrance of the old egocentric self, not fully developed, but rather in the process of being formed.

John Coburn points out that Jesus never mentioned His death without also mentioning His resurrection. The two processes occur side by side within us. As we die to self, we are being reborn to a new life in Christ. It just happens without effort when we trust ourselves to a power beyond ourselves.

☙☙☙

February 25, 1985

"Let Christ be formed in me and let me learn of Him all lowliness of heart, all gentleness of bearing, all modesty of speech, all helpfulness of action and promptness in doing my Father's will." Amen.

☙☙☙

February 26, 1985

A phrase in yesterday's sermon really struck home: "It's more important to be loving than to be right." How I like to be right and to have others acknowledge that I am right! I want to be seen as bright, intelligent, and capable. Of course I would also like to be seen as loving. But which do I want more? When I insist on my way it is often at the expense of others who may see things more clearly, or from a different perspective. What prompts me is often a matter of self-esteem. This is the Pharisee in me.

I often do kind and generous acts but how often are they prompted by love? Are they done to be seen and praised? Would I be as kind and generous if no one was aware of my good deeds? As I probe for answers to these questions, I realize how far short I am of "loving my neighbor as myself." My prayer is: "Help me, Lord, to be more like the Publican than the Pharisee."

ᛉᛉᛉ

March 19, 1985

The early Christians had worked out no theological dogma, had no creed and were not bound by Jewish legalism. Their one overriding contention was that

Jesus, whom they had known and loved, was the Christ. They had seen Him put to death, but now they knew that in some miraculous way He had been restored to them. This was all they needed to know. It gave them faith and courage and overwhelming joy. Nothing the world did to them could take away this inner certainty. Perhaps this is all Christians ever need—an unshakeable faith that Jesus is Christ, the Savior of the world. He becomes our personal Savior when we willingly and joyfully commit ourselves and all that we have to Him.

I'm beginning to see that my deep-seated desire to understand, and to rationalize the gospel story has been a deterrent to my faith. Jesus said: "Except you become as little children you shall not enter the kingdom of heaven." I wonder if the "journey into Christ" is not a journey back to childhood. Is it a matter of dispossessing ourselves of our intellectual pretensions and our desire to understand?

I am pursuing a new line of thought—perhaps not thought so much as experience. I must believe that "the Spirit leads us into all truth," even though it takes a lifetime to arrive.

✿ ✿ ✿

March 25, 1985

The story of the Prodigal Son is the story of a young man who wanted to be independent of his father. We are told that after wasting his inheritance he found himself in a strange country having to feed pigs. He finally "comes to himself" and decides to return home. He repents and turns back, acknowledging that the self he had been indulging was not his true self. The independence he sought separated him from his father's love. But in returning home he found forgiveness and acceptance. In the story, the change that took place is not specified but we can imagine that once he found himself enveloped in his father's love the son discovered who he truly was.

ﭏﭏﭏ

April 2, 1985—Tuesday in Holy Week

"Oh Jerusalem, Oh Jerusalem!"
When Jesus comes in sight of the city that was the center of Judaism, the site of the great temple dedicated to the worship of God, He wept. It was heartbreaking for Him to see the corruption, the greed, and the graft that permeated the city's life and, indeed, the life of Judaism itself.

As I read these words of lamentation which Jesus spoke as He looked down on this place which had so often rejected the prophets, this place where He was soon to meet His own death, I can feel the terrible surge of love and longing which He must have felt.

As we look out on our world, our nation, our city, should we not feel the same surge of grief over how little we have allowed God to rule our lives? Never, it seems, has there been such widespread warfare—so much of it in the name of religion. Famine exists in huge areas of Africa, while persecution, torture, and injustice is the norm in many countries. We in America are blessed with peace and prosperity, but instead of turning to God in gratitude for our blessings and dedicating our wealth to others less fortunate than us, we have become materialistic and self-serving as a nation.

I believe Jesus must still weep over the world He was sent to save. And for those of us who try to identify our lives with His, we must share His grief and at the same time, recognize and confess our complicity and guilt for the evil that exists. "Thy Kingdom come, O God, Thy rule, O Christ, begin; break with thine iron rod the tyranny of sin." Amen.

ᚹᚹᚹ

April 30, 1985

Last night in the Bible study group we discussed John 10:10-20, where Jesus describes himself as the Good Shepherd who cares for his sheep. I had never before thought about being a sheep and if I had I would have resisted the idea. Sheep are stupid, they go where they are led and take no responsibility for themselves or for their comrades. The good shepherd is the one who cares for them, who seeks for the lost, and who knows where they are going.

A sermon Sunday emphasized that Christians have the role of shepherds. We are given the task of caring for each other and of bringing others into the fold. In another sermon I heard exactly the opposite view was set forth. The preacher extolled the joys of being sheep. He told how in his younger days he wanted to achieve something of significance and aspired to a position of importance. After years of wrestling, he finally heard a voice say to him: "Do what you are doing. I love and accept you just as you are; you don't have to change the world; trust me." With these words a burden was removed and he became a very successful minister to the deaf.

My conclusion, as I think about these two different interpretations of the same story, is that we must be both sheep and shepherd—we need to be nurtured, but we also are called to nurture others.

ᴘᴘᴘ

May 10, 1985

The vestry retreat was a "Mountain Top" experience both literally and figuratively. Fourteen members of St. Paul's vestry gathered at a Conference Center high up in the Blue Ridge Mountains. We were a very diverse group in lifestyle, in theology, and in spiritual awareness. Some participants from the business community were chiefly interested in the budget, others primarily in religious education for their children. A number admitted that the closest they ever felt God's presence was in the beauty of the natural world and in the love they felt for their families.

We spent our evening expressing spiritual gifts by making posters, drawing pictures, and writing poems. Each in turn had to explain what it was they considered their most important gift. We all enjoyed exploring our differences as well as what we had in common. The following morning, under a brilliant blue sky, we celebrated the Eucharist on top of the highest hill. It was a time to transcend our differences *and unite in a spirit of fellowship.*

The reason I chose to write about this event is how much it helped me to accept people who think differently from me, understanding that for the most part, we are each the product of our early family life, our education, and our careers. I no longer need to pass judgment. Everyone does their best according to the gifts that have been given them.

᠊᠊᠊

June 6, 1985

Last Saturday Bob and I celebrated our 50th wedding anniversary. For three full days we had all our family with us. The children, and grandchildren too, had planned a banquet with so many wonderful surprises. Messages from friends as well as cards and gifts; T-shirts with "June 1st" on the front, a skit, and a song, "You're the Tops," to which they had composed their own special words. So much preparation and loving labor had gone into making it an ever-memorable event. We are indeed blessed beyond our deserving by this wonderful family. We have often failed, but through the grace of God, we must have done something right.

I have had a full and wonderful marriage. There

have been failures, misunderstandings, and disappointments, but we never failed in our love for each other. I look to the years ahead to bring us even closer and to God who has united us and whom we seek to serve. My heart overflows with gratitude.

ᛊᛊᛊ

June 18, 1985

"Why O Lord, is it so hard for me to let go?" Is it because I don't trust others to carry on as I think they should? Is it because I don't have faith in the guidance of your Holy Sprit as manifested in others? Or is my vanity involved? I still like to be seen as a "mover" and achiever, one who gets things done.

For the past five years I have been very active—Vestry, Walk-In Ministry as well as caring for my family. I have been afforded many opportunities to exert what gifts I have. I think it's time to quit. I think God is calling me to a different role, one where I willingly and cheerfully relinquish the reigns and take a back seat. It's the role of Mary rather than Martha, which I now seek—or, for which I am sought.

ᛊᛊᛊ

June 22, 1985

"Jesus awoke and rebuked the wind and said to the sea 'Peace, be still.' And the wind ceased and there was a great calm."

Thursday with the Walk-In Ministry was a hectic day. I felt pushed and pulled in all directions. More than once I lost patience. Looking back I wish I had paused and taken a few quiet minutes to recollect myself and to listen to Jesus' voice saying "Peace, be still." I needed the calm that comes from withdrawing from immediate pressures and remembering in whose Name I'm doing this ministry.

July 3, 1985

Yesterday I resigned as coordinator of the Walk-in Ministry. I shall miss it in many ways. For five years it's taken up a great deal of my time and energy but it has also had many rewards. I've come into contact with people so unlike myself and yet some of them have become my friends.

But I'm tired of the responsibility and my successor will bring other gifts to the role of coordinator. The underlying reason, however, is a strong feeling that I need to become a more passive and receiving person. As far as I am able to determine, the Spirit is leading me in a new direction. There are discoveries I need to make which I can only do in returning and rest: I am eager to find out what lies ahead.

ᴈᴈᴈ

July 3, 1989

A prayer this morning reads: "Lord, I often see the necklace, but not the string that holds it together. Lord, help me to know the thread of your love that runs through my life and holds it all together."

I think that this is a wonderful analogy. The daily events of our lives are the beads—some big, some small, some beautiful, but most having no obvious significance. Each bead is unique and doesn't seem to relate to the one before or after it. However, when threaded together they are integrated into one unbroken string. The first bead and the last bead close a circle firmly joined by a clasp.

In retrospect I can see the thread of God's love which has run through my life and given meaning to seemingly unrelated and inconsequential happenings. When every bead is finally in place they will form a complete circle and I shall find myself back at my beginning, firmly held in the clasp of God's hands.

᷾᷾᷾

August 1, 1989

Another hostage was put to death yesterday in Beirut despite all the prayers that have been offered for their safety and release.

It raises many questions in my mind. Have the prayers had any effect either on the hostages or their captors? Or is the only benefit on those of us who pray? Perhaps in praying we become more compassionate and more conscious of the pain and fear felt by others. I just don't know, but still I feel called upon to offer intercession, even for people I may never know. I believe this is God's will and somehow, unbeknownst to us, He does heed our prayers.

᷾᷾᷾

August 10, 1989

For the past three months the meditations in FORWARD DAY BY DAY have been addressed to "Dear Seeker" supposing there is something of the seeker in all of us. I feel sure that I, for one, will go to my grave still seeking assurances which I trust will be revealed in the world-to-come, whatever that may be.

ᛣᛣᛣ

October 26, 1989

In recent months I have experienced a lack of spiritual awareness and a disinclination to pray. I attend my Prayer Group, but more from a sense of obligation than from desire. I have been questioning the value of intercessory prayer. Of late I've been praying for a son whose condition seems not to improve.

I know that the soul's journey often takes one through periods of darkness and dryness when it is only a matter of discipline and perseverance. There are no delightful coincidences such as I have known; no sense of direction and no undergirding conviction; all we can do is just "hang in there" until the road takes a turn and light is restored. What is needed, what I especially need at this time, is some outside spiritual nurturing. I have so often found the help and guidance I sought in books, sermons, and people with whom to share my journey. For the moment I have found none of these.

ᛣᛣᛣ

October 31, 1989

Psalm 44 begins: "Awake O Lord, why are you sleeping?" It speaks of God's apparent absence when we call upon Him. Where is God when we need Him most? I don't think He is playing "hide and go seek" with us just to test us.

I am reminded of the "importunate widow" who sought bread from her neighbor. But I don't think we need to implore God. He knows our needs better than we do ourselves.

Perhaps He just wants us to rest, to take a break from striving and, when we are ready, to come back to Him refreshed. Instead of asking anything, it would please Him, I'm sure, if we would only thank Him for past blessings and for accepting us even in a state of alienation. His love will never let us go beyond His reach.

꙰ ꙰ ꙰

November 11, 1989

Yesterday I spent a quiet hour in the chapel of a local retreat center. It had been a long time since I'd been there. I went looking for reassurance and confirmation; a desire to find myself in God's presence. And I wasn't disappointed. Nothing dramatic occurred but as I let myself float I was aware of a spiritual reality—of an ambiance derived, I believe, from all the prayers and devotions which had taken place within these walls. I got the impression that I was being upheld and affirmed by a multitude of unknown Christians, both past and present. There seemed to exist a communion among us which transcends time.

Then the thought arose that, if past prayers lingered in this place and could reach out to those of us in the present, so, too, could the prayers we were now offering be used by God to benefit those who, in the future, may come here seeking renewal and guidance.

☙☙☙

February 25, 1990

Tomorrow I go to the hospital to have a knee replacement. I suspect it will be painful and uncomfortable and a part of me dreads it. I might even call it off if it weren't too late. On the other hand I know of many people who will be praying for me, and this will, I'm sure, ease my apprehension and hasten my recovery. It happened 22 years ago when I had a mastectomy, so I'm counting on it happening again. God's Spirit will provide the strength and patience I will need. Jesus will be present whether or not I'm aware of Him. This can be the time to renew and deepen my faith. I pray this will be so.

ᵏᵖ ᵏᵖ ᵏᵖ

March 27, 1990

So much to be thankful for! My recovery continues and I daily feel stronger and in less pain. Total recovery has taken longer than I expected. However, these weeks of convalescence have been rewarding. I've learned to be patient and I've experienced so much love and kindness. By far the greatest blessing has been Bob's unfailing care. We have drawn closer together these past few weeks than we've been in years. I think we've both come to realize how precious our days are together. Nothing else is nearly as important.

ᵏᵖ ᵏᵖ ᵏᵖ

October 2, 1990

Bob died of a sudden heart attack on Sept. 21st. The day before he had not felt well, but neither of us thought his condition serious. Friday morning he awoke with pain in his chest. I called the doctor and we headed for the hospital. On the way Bob said, "You don't need to drive so fast." Those were the last words I heard him speak. He was taken to the emergency room in a wheel chair while I parked the car. By the time I returned my dear beloved husband was dead. No goodbye or last loving words.

I was stunned. It was incredible that he had left me so totally unprepared. But for Bob it was the best of all possible ways to go. He would have hated feeling ill, infirm and dependent on others. We had a long and happy marriage, blessed with four wonderful children, five grandchildren with a sixth soon to be born. Life goes on. But it will be a very different life for me. I couldn't face it on my own but thank God, I won't have to.

ᴘᴘᴘ

October 12, 1990

If, in God's perspective, "A thousand ages are like an evening gone," does it not also follow that space, like time, is infinite? It cannot be measured by inches, yards, or even miles. In the realm of the Spirit there are no boundaries. We can be near our loved ones whether they are trillions of miles away or in the next room. All we need do is reach out to them.

When Bob was living I would enter this room each morning, closing the door to keep him from entering. Now, though I still close the door, I call him to come in and share with me the peace and stillness of God's presence.

There are times when I sensed that the curtain which separates this world from the next is a very flimsy one which can be raised sufficiently to give us a glimpse of that "Land of light and joy" in communion with the saints who have already entered.

ᛤᛤᛤ

November 5, 1990

In Ecclesiasticus, chapter 38, the author offers this advice:

"My son, shed tears over a dead man and intone the lament to show your grief. Observe the mourning the dead deserve. One day, or two to avoid comment, and then be comforted in your sorrow; for grief can lead to death, a grief-stricken heart undermines your strength. Do not forget there is no going back; you cannot help the dead and you will harm yourself. Once the dead man is laid to rest, let his memory rest too. Do not fret for him, once his spirit departs."

What amazing advice to have been written so long ago.

I am trying to overcome grief as I know it is unproductive and keeps me feeling sorry for myself and prevents my living fully in the present. I don't, however, think that we should "Let his memory rest, too." I want to remember all the joyful times Bob and I had together. Memory is a gift that should be preserved as long as possible.

For my own part, I am in a sense starting a new life. I am free to make choices and must, whether I want to or not, make decisions about my future. I am now wholly responsible for what I make of each day. I begin each morning by asking God for the guidance of his Holy Spirit. He has so far given me a degree of faith and courage to face the future unafraid and that "all will be well."

❦ ❦ ❦

November 6, 1990

"Blessed are those who mourn for they shall be comforted." As I understand the word comfort, it means strength, not ease. Those who mourn are made strong. How this happens I do not know, but I do know that I have experienced a source of strength outside myself during these weeks of mourning. Perhaps it's not from the outside but from inside myself—the work of the indwelling spirit. To mourn is to feel a sense of loss, of incompleteness, of brokenness. These are the conditions in which we admit our insufficiency and are open to God's grace. And God is always more ready to give than we to receive. He is just waiting for us to cry "help."

Psalm 62. "He alone is my rock and my salvation, my stronghold, so that I shall not be greatly shaken."

𝒦𝒦𝒦

January 1, 1991

"Each of us is born to become ourselves." The concept that life is a "becoming" is not new to me. The question is: Who or what are we becoming? When we were conceived was there already an image of who we were meant to become? Does God know of the ultimate person we shall be? How does our end tie up with our beginning?

A year has ended and another begun. Does this annual passage of time have a corresponding meaning in our personal lives? I have intimations that as I approach the last years of my life, I'm being offered, each day, a new beginning with wonderful possibilities. It is only with the grace of God that I can attain them.

ΚΟΚΟΚΟ

February 28, 1991

Psalm 19:12. "Who can tell how he offends? Cleanse me from my secret faults."

I am aware of many of my faults but what about my secret ones? Are there faults which I keep hidden even from myself? God, who knows the secrets of our hearts, surely knows what they are. Perhaps He keeps them hidden from us until we are courageous enough to face them. He doesn't want us overwhelmed with a sense of sin and failure and so He discloses to us, bit by bit, our shortcomings insofar as we are able to bear them. We can only work to overcome our sins one at a time, otherwise we might give up in despair.

What is the one fault I must work on this Lent? It is, I think, a lack of humility and a desire for recognition and appreciation. How do I go about becoming humble? First, it is to accept all things as grace. As St. Paul said, "Not I but Christ working in me." I deserve no credit for anything I do, or am, because it is the work of the Holy Spirit.

ΚΟΚΟΚΟ

April 17, 1991

I've just come in from a walk. This is an unusually beautiful night. A tiny crescent moon sits in the western sky and underneath the planet Venus shines brightly. The afterglow from the sunset casts a rosy glow over the pond. Small birds flit from tree to tree getting settled for the approaching night. The fragrance of wisteria permeates all. It is a rare moment of being totally absorbed in the enchantment which surrounds me.

This has been a lovely spring, dogwood and azaleas blooming in profusion. It seems as if nature is conspiring to make it hard for me to leave this place, or, perhaps, she is doing her best to put on an unforgettable display that I shall remember for many springs to come.

ϗϗϗ

June 26, 1991

I have a strong feeling that each day of my life I am one day closer to whatever it is that God wants me to become. I hope I am not mistaken.

ϗϗϗ

July 25, 1991

There is a Nigerian saying: "It is the heart that gives, the fingers just let go."

As I'm preparing to move, there is so much in my life that I must just "let go." I have enjoyed making gifts to my friends, matching the gift to the recipient. It is hard parting with heirlooms and things with sentimental value. I want to pass on to my children and grandchildren pieces of furniture and silver which I have inherited from my ancestors.

When one gives with the heart the gift is relinquished joyfully, expecting nothing, not even thanks in return. "It is more blessed to give rather than to receive."

Help me, dear God, to give generously without calculation, of all that has been entrusted to my care. Amen.

ĶͰĶͰĶͰ

August 8, 1991

I have just come across a meditation entitled "Sans Cire." Translated from French this means "without varnish or veneer." It is from these words that we get our English words "sincere." To be sincere is to be absolutely genuine; to strip off the facade behind which most of us hide. It is to allow people to know us as we really are.

Another quote from the same author (Fr. Andrew): "The pilgrimage of the soul is a progress from and to and with and through. It is a journeying from self to God; it is with Christ, and it is through the mystical stages of prayer in which the Holy Spirit is our guide. Our life is a great adventure, a romance, a quest which was started by God himself."

Dear God, I pray that your Holy Spirit may continue to guide me, not only in my spiritual journey but in my journey to my new house. It is going to be hard to leave this one where I have lived for 32 years, leaving behind people and places I have loved. I want to perceive the move as a great adventure opening up new paths and new possibilities for me to pursue. Amen.

ᛞᛞᛞ

November 8, 1991

I've been thinking a lot about courage since coming to this place. I doubt there are many people who ever think that a retirement home is a place to discover courage in daily life. It's only as I associate with my fellow residents, observe their conduct, learn something of their background, that I begin to realize what each has had to overcome—bereavement, suffering, helplessness, loneliness, loss of sight and loss of hearing. Perhaps the worst thing for many is the realization of creeping disability, mental and physical.

And yet the atmosphere is cheerful and bright. It is also compassionate. There is always a helping hand and words of encouragement. Very few complain. Backs may be bent but spirits are high. Faith, hope, and love abound.

ଡ଼ଡ଼ଡ଼

November 20, 1991

The fall issue of IONA DAYBOOK deals with various aspects of growing old. It reminds us that ripening takes place in the natural world and so does dying. Autumn is a time to reflect on our own mortality.

Yesterday's reading was from the French psychologist, Paul Tournier, in which he spoke of an inner, as well as an outer change that takes place as we increase in years. It is one from action to inaction. In the East this process is called "wei-wei," that is 'non-acting!' Tournier goes on to speak of "the grace granted when we let go." Through acceptance we find a "secure peace which is not of this world, that is the detachment necessary for a happy old age. We do not forsake the claims the world has upon us, rather, we forsake our desires and our wills for the material things of this world."

Dear God, Heavenly Father, help me to attain this kind of detachment that my will may be Your will and Your will be mine. Amen.

የ የ የ

July 3, 1992

As I approach the last page of this journal, I think this may well be my final entry. I have lost the incentive to continue an account of my spiritual journey. I don't mean that this is the end of the journey, which I pray will continue as long as I live.

I began journaling some forty years ago, at a time when I was lonely and have kept at it intermittently ever since. Reading back over old entries, I see how I have changed and I also see a pattern that has emerged to give meaning to the events of my life.

I started writing for myself alone, but subconsciously I may have been hoping that a record of my journey might, in some way, be an encouragement to others to do the same. At this time I see no prospect of that happening.

ΚΟΚΟΚΟ

October 31, 1992

Among the delights we encounter on our spiritual journeys are coincidences. So often when we are depressed, discouraged, and in need of encouragement to keep on seeking God's guidance, an answer will appear when we least expect it—in a book, or a headline in the daily newspaper.

Lately I have been feeling dispirited and have little incentive to continue my journal. And then, out of the blue, I happened upon a book by Henri Nouwen called THE ROAD TO DAYBREAK. It is a journal of the year he spent in Trosly, France, seeking God's guidance in determining the future course his life should take. In the opening chapter he says he heard "Something like an inner voice telling me to start keeping a journal again." For the past four years he had not done so, but now he decides, "There is no better way to keep in touch with God's work in me than by recording what is happening to me day after day."

So, here I have not only the answer to my own

question about continuing a journal, but a wonderful source of spiritual nurturing as well.

ᴻᴻᴻ

December 12, 1992

Today's reading in the IONA DAYBOOK is a poem, called "Groping: A Time to Stay Put." It contains the thought that the "Best journey is made inward. It is the interior that calls."

For the past 80 years I have led a very active life and have traveled far more extensively than most people. Now the time has come "to stay put." To a lesser or greater extent, travel is a form of escape. It is a diversion from the everyday sameness of life. It is life where you are limited by circumstances and within the scope of 'given' relationships, that we are called to live.

Of late I've been thinking a lot about patience and waiting, this seems to me to be the Advent message. We are called to wait the coming of the Lord. To wait, not thoughtlessly or passively, but hopefully, expectantly, and purposefully. The world is the Lord's. He created it, and us, for his purpose. It still seems a long way off, but if He can wait, hopefully, for the coming of His Kingdom, so can we. There are areas in our lives where we can make a difference, even though few of us can change the course of history. We need faith, as well as patience while we wait.

ᛍᛍᛍ

December 15, 1992

Winter is the season of stripping bare, of diminishment—the trees lose their leaves; the days are shorter and the sun is less bright.

It is a season when God, the Almighty, Creator of Heaven and Earth, diminished Himself to become a new born babe, stripped of His power and glory, vulnerable and weak, at the mercy of the very world which He created. The only attribute, which he retained, was His love, and that was His very being.

O God, strip me of all vain desires, of all my ego needs for satisfaction, appreciation, and affection. Take away all that keeps me from loving you with my whole heart and others as myself. At the service this evening open my heart wider and deeper than ever before to that love which became incarnate with the birth of a baby on that first Christmas morning. That would be the greatest gift I could receive and should be the only one I desire. Amen.

ᛍᛍᛍ

January 1, 1993

The year began for me with a glorious sunrise. Awake at six, I watched for over an hour as the colors—first intense cobalt blue, coral, and gray faded to pale turquoise, pink, and saffron as the sun's rays became less oblique. Exactly at 7:30 the sun, a brilliant orange ball, appeared on the horizon.

My thought as I watched this grand spectacle was "The heavens are declaring the glory of God!" And my prayer was that this might be an omen for a happy, peaceful year ahead and that God's glory might reach out and embrace all of His creation.

(Hymn 5) "Oh splendor of God's glory bright, O Thou that bringest light from light/All laud to God, the Father be, all praise eternal Son to Thee/All glory to the Spirit raise/In equal and unending praise."

ꕤꕤꕤ

February 10, 1993

"Love does not find its fullness in achieving complete non-detachment. Love's deepest realization is found in growing, struggling, moving, longing, reaching toward perfection, while living life fully in the here and now."

I picture my life as a line stretched between two

poles. One pole represents contentment, acceptance of where I am and what I am. The other pole on which my life depends is my search for understanding, my desire to be the person I'm meant to be; my regrets for past failures and a longing for a better world— not for myself but for all people.

Must there always be this tension or, as my life grows shorter, does the space between the two poles diminish and I become reconciled to the fact that only God can bridge the gap.

ᛕᛕᛕ

March 3, 1993

Last night in a class I've been attending each member was asked to give a symbol for Lent. My first reply was, "The vine." Jesus said, "I am the vine, without me you can do nothing." Without my attachment to Jesus all my efforts would be fruitless.

My second thought was pruning shears. Lent is a time to trim out of our lives all those things which are superfluous and which prevent us from being completely dependent on the vine—things like pride, vanity, self-indulgence, jealousy, etc., but until we can prune these faults from our lives we will be unable to bear fruit.

Henri Nouwen had this same thought in mind when he wrote: "It helps me to think of loneliness, feelings of inner darkness and despair and the lack of human affection as God's pruning. When confronted with the painful experiences common to us all, I must learn to accept them as evidence of God's work in me drawing me closer to Himself."

ကြ ကြ ကြ

March 19, 1993

I have signed on to a three-day retreat at Holy Cross Monastery. I was there two years ago, soon after Bob's death. Then I was trying to sort out my life and plan for the future. My purpose now is to delve deeper into my relationship with God and seek His will for my remaining years.

Before setting out on this venture I know I need to prepare myself, to empty myself of all lesser desires so that I may be open to his Spirit. How do I pray to achieve this goal?

From what I have been reading (Henri Nouwen and Evelyn Underhill) I get the idea that worship and adoration are the way to approach God—not too much introspection and reasoned thought. I find it difficult to become self-forgetful and focus all my attention on God. I often start my morning prayer by saying, "Bless the Lord, O my soul and forget not all his benefits," which helps set the tone for what follows.

According to Nouwen there are three necessary elements to prayer: "Reaching up to God, reaching down into oneself and reaching out to others." The reaching up to God must proceed the other two. Jesus' own prayer was not limited to glorifying His Father in heaven. He began by asking that God's Name be hallowed, but continued to ask for more mundane things—food, forgiveness and deliverance from temptation.

"True worshipers shall worship the Father in spirit and in truth, for the Father seeketh such to worship him." I pray that I shall learn to do this with "all my heart and with all my mind and with all my soul."

℘℘℘

March 29, 1993

I am here at the Abbey and have just attended Vespers. The chanting of the monks is, I think, the purest form of worship that there is.

Last night before going to bed my eye caught sight of the Crucifix on the opposite wall. Some impulse *made me take it down. I think I wanted to see if it was handcarved wood or just molded plastic. The next thing I knew I had the Crucifix cradled in my arms, loving it and protecting it as I might a baby. It was such an uncharacteristic thing for me to do that I felt embarrassed and quickly returned it to the hook on which it hung. But just for a few seconds while holding it, I felt a warm love flooding my heart—a love for Jesus who had once, for my sake and for the world's, hung upon a cross.*

March 31, 1993

My last day at the Abbey. I came with the desire to explore new dimensions of worship and adoration. I think I was seeking some "wholly other" experience—the moth for the star sort of thing. I have been led to discover that worship is not entirely otherworldly. It is not done at a safe distance but involves our whole being. It's more like an embrace than a bow.

My experience with the crucifix was an epiphany. It told me that God wants us to come as close as possible to the crucified Christ, to feel His pain and to know the suffering which, for love's sake, He endured.

The book which I brought along to read urges those on retreat to imagine scenes from Jesus' life in which they are present. In so doing we cease to be onlookers and become participants. All this ties together two apparently unrelated concerns of mine. The first one is to deepen my sense of worship while the second is concern for all the pain that exists in the world. In Christ on the cross the two are joined. The God we worship is the God who suffers for His creation and He invites, but does not coerce us, to share His pain. It's an invitation I would rather not accept, but if I wish to follow Jesus, I seem to have little choice.

Contemplative prayer may seem to remove us from the harsh realities of our own everyday world as we seek to come closer to God. But God is not remote from the world's pain. He's in the midst of it. And so, if we are to worship God "In spirit and in truth," we cannot remain aloof and otherworldly.

℘ ℘ ℘

May 14, 1993

At a recent Conference the leader was Dr. James Fenhagen. His subject was the "Spirituality of Diminishment," and he referred to the words of John the Baptist: "I must decrease that He may increase."

As with John, we must all find our own personhood before we can relinquish it. Diminishment is both voluntary and involuntary. Some things are taken from us in the course of growing old; others we surrender of our own volition. Material things, certainly. The older we get the less we need or want, and, we become aware that "We can't take them with us."

More difficult to relinquish are our opinions, our prejudices, our desires, and, finally, our wills. But there can be a plus side to this. We attain a freedom which we could never have when who and what we are depended on our possessions and on our own abilities. At last we learn to depend wholly on God for our identity and our accomplishments.

ᛰᛰᛰ

June 3, 1993

I've been thinking about the "grace of extravagance" (my own expression). What I mean by this is uncalculated generosity—giving without counting the cost or expecting a reward.

My granddaughter gave her mother for her birthday fifty long-stemmed red roses. It could be seen as a foolish expenditure for a teenager on an allowance, but it was her way of expressing her love and gratitude for all her mother meant to her.

I am reminded of the woman who anointed Jesus' feet with precious ointment. When Judas reprimanded her for "wasting" money needlessly, Jesus' response was, "What this woman has done will be remembered always," and so it has been!

ΚΡΚΡΚΡ

August 26, 1993

"A Journey Towards Contentment."

This is a title which I'm considering for my memoirs which I am in the process of writing. But first, I must feel confident that this is the story of my life. Have I really been seeking contentment all these years and if so, what do I have in mind and is it a worthwhile goal?

There is, I believe, a difference between contentment and satisfaction. I shall never be satisfied with myself or my life. But being content is coming to terms with all that has happened, knowing there's nothing I can change, regretting my failures but accepting my limitations in the same way that God accepts them.

What I most desire is my children's happiness and

well-being. For the remainder of my life I want to give them gifts which they will enjoy.

Contentment in old age is surely worth pursuing, but it is not the only goal that I desire.

ᏦᏦᏦ

January 17, 1994

Peace! How often we say it and how little meaning we attach to it. "Passing the peace" in church is usually little more than a handshake or a quick hug. What is it that we are really wishing our neighbor when we say: "The peace of the Lord be with you," if in fact we say the words at all.

The peace of the Lord—what did Jesus know of peace that He would share it with us? In His world, as in ours, there was little outward peace. But He said, "Peace I leave with you; my peace I give to you. I do not give as the world gives." And again: "Do not let your hearts be troubled, and do not let them be afraid."

The peace of the Lord comes from entrusting our lives and all that we do to God's care. It keeps us from anxiety and fear. Peace is a gift that gives us confidence and serenity to accept ourselves and the circumstances of our lives. This takes a great burden from us and gives us new energy and new faith to live our daily lives.

Dear Lord, I pray for your peace in my heart. Your peace is beyond my understanding—it is a gift of the highest order and is not dependent on anything I do. All that is required is to say, "Thank you."

⫷⫸⫷

February 7, 1994

Hebrews 13:14 "For you have no lasting city, but we are looking forward to the city that is to come."

The question of a life beyond this one has been much on my mind lately. Is there really a "city that is to come?" and what will it be like to inhabit such a city? Without our physical bodies shall we be able to recognize those we've known and loved in this world? I suspect these are questions no one can answer until the time comes—perhaps on the point of death, perhaps not then.

I have been searching for some confirmation that my beloved Bob still exists in some recognizable form. In my imagination and in my longing I want to see him, or at least feel his presence as I remember him, i.e., flesh and blood. But that part of him was reduced to ashes. So what remains? Remembering back to the time of his death, I'm sure that what kept me from despair was the thought of someday being reunited. But how?

In St. John's gospel Jesus says to his disciples: "A little while and you will no longer see me and again, a little while and you will see me." And just a few moments later, "But I will see you again and your hearts will rejoice and no one will take your joy from you."

Surely Jesus was not referring to a physical, but a spiritual reunion with His disciples. Even if He appeared to them in bodily form after the resurrection, it was only for a short period of time. After His Ascension He did not appear physically— even Paul only heard a voice.

Somewhere else Jesus is quoted as saying "Lo, I am with you always." Can this be said of those we love who've gone before us? I surely hope so.

℘℘℘

February 12, 1994

"In the end, it is our own wholeness we must seek, and the only possible creation is ourselves." This quotation seems on the surface to be too concerned with self, when Jesus teaches that we must lose our selves in order to find them.

The meditation suggests that the reason we dread old age is that it comes with the realization of how incomplete our lives have been. We have failed to live up to the hopes and expectations which we held in our youth. Our accomplishments have fallen far short of our aspirations. But the author insists that our one and only goal should be our own creation (or, should I say re-creation?).

Old age gives us opportunities denied us in our busy, active lives. More time to reflect, to get our priorities in order, more opportunities to seek out the sick and lonely, more time alone.

Recently, I heard it said that, "The longest journey we will ever embark on is the journey from head to heart." From the desire to understand to the desire to love and adore. This is a journey I'll try to make during the coming weeks of Lent. I don't think this is what the author had in mind when he spoke of "creating ourselves," but to follow the dictates of my heart will, I believe, lead to wholeness.

St. Augustine said, "Thou hast made us for Yourself and our hearts are restless till they find their rest in Thee."

𐤊𐤊𐤊

February 23, 1994

Alongside the journey from "head to heart" is the journey from obligation to desire, from will to want, from law to grace. There comes a time (and I hope that I have reached it) when all that I undertake and do is prompted by love and thankfulness rather than from a sense of duty.

Lenten discipline is just such an exercise. This year I have given up a pre-dinner drink because I WANT to, not because I OUGHT to. I hope it pleases God that I have done so, but in a certain sense I've done it for myself.

The same motivation applies to the giving of gifts and charitable contributions. I give because I desire to do so. I am trying to learn to do so without wanting or expecting credit. One can give without loving but one can't love without giving.

ﻉﻉﻉ

June 23, 1994

"The meaning is in the waiting." This is the last line of a poem by R. S. Thomas.

Please, dear Lord, may I wait in patience and in faith for Your word to me this day.

God's word is not always a spoken word. It can

take various forms: a sense of well-being, an opportunity to serve, a call from a friend, a thing of beauty, or, perhaps, the memory of a past blessing.

I am often too impatient with God, forgetting that His time is not our time. Waiting, I feel sure, is a necessary discipline and in it I shall try to find meaning. Here is a poem by Mark Van Doren.

"Waiting"
To wait within is hardest;
To be, while still becoming;
Doomed to all that slowness
Never once to die.
To wait until tomorrow
Costs but a little sleep.
The wilderness inward
Takes years to cross.
Nor is the going wasted
If every stretch were loved.
The last hill then is home ground
Though all its light be strange.

🙥🙥🙥

March 30, 1995

I'm sitting at my window looking out toward the

Washington Monument and the great city that lies all around it. From here it is beautiful and peaceful, but I know that close up every kind of crime and evil are present. How sad that this great national Capital should be the scene of so much corruption, greed, meanness and injustice. I think of Jesus' lament over Jerusalem; I feel sure He still grieves over the cities of the world. I can only share His sorrow and offer my prayers for all—rich and poor, good and evil, powerful and powerless—that they may find redemption in God's enduring love.

ᛣᛣᛣ

July 7, 1995

The sermon today was based on the story of Martha and Mary. It was presented as a skit depicting Mary in deep conversation with Jesus while Martha scurried about doing chores. Finally, her indignation at Mary's idleness boiled over. She interrupted Mary and Jesus, demanding that Jesus tell her sister to come and give her a hand.

I could so well identify with the situation, remembering many occasions when I felt I was being put upon. I could almost recapture the resentment and self-pity I have experienced when left alone to do the work when others were doing as they pleased.

Much as I would prefer to identify with Mary, it is not my nature to leave beds unmade or dishes unwashed. My work ethic tells me to first get the chores done before taking time to "sit at Jesus' feet." I can, on the other hand, understand Mary's impatience. Here was the opportunity of a lifetime that Martha was missing.

Most of us are made up of equal parts of Martha and Mary—sometimes one and sometimes the other. That's O.K. as long as neither is judgmental or resentful towards the other.

Dear Lord, help me to keep a proper balance between my prayer life and my daily round of activities. I think they are both of value and neither one should occupy all my time and attention. What I really want is for my activities to be consistent with my prayers. Actually my activities at times are in greater accord with Jesus' teachings than are my unruly thoughts which too often, like Martha's, are centered on myself. Right now, what I hear Jesus saying to me is "Go to bed. Tomorrow is another day."

ﻙﻙﻙ

July 25, 1995

In the "Cloud of Unknowing" I came across this: "Your whole life now must be one of longing—and this longing must be in the depth of your will, put there by God with your consent."

For years I have felt this longing which God has put in my heart but it's not yet in the "depth of my will."

For as long as I can remember I have tried to explore the mystery which is God with my mind. Now I think I'm being led to accept it without question, live with it and trust myself to the Spirit's guidance. Ever since Bob's death and moving here, I've had a feeling there's something more God wants of my life. Still the question keeps arising: what and why?

I spoke to Liz today about starting spiritual direction. At times I question myself and my motives. Why am I launching out into the unknown at my age? Am I making too much of my spiritual journey? What makes it special and worth examining? Always, questions and not many answers.

☙☙☙

July 26, 1995

To live more fully in God's love and in His service demands more discipline and sacrifice than I've ever been willing to undertake. I am quite adept at living in two worlds at the same time. I want to be with God, but I'm reluctant to give up worldly pleasures. I spend far too much time considering what I shall wear and what I shall eat, even who I will befriend. I have attempted to fast but not in a disciplined way.

Too long have I straddled a fence not wanting to wholeheartedly commit myself, enjoying the fruits of both worlds.

ᛣᛣᛣ

July 31, 1995

"For God alone my soul in silence waits." (Psalm 62)

This sense of longing for God is as old as the hills. He must have put this longing for Himself in our hearts when He created us. I've just sat for fifteen minutes repeating, "For Thee alone my soul in silence waits." In a quiet, unremarkable way I experienced a sense of Presence—no lights or voices, just the quiet. It seems to me that God leaves the big epiphanies for very special times in our lives. Meantime, with our consent we are being gradually stripped of whatever stands between us and the "us" He would have us become. All this goes on in the stillness when we open all the doors and windows and invite the Holy Spirit into the usually well-guarded sanctuary of our inner being.

There are times when I worry that I'm not being truly led along the path I have chosen—that it is only in my imagination that I'm called to explore deeper and deeper the life of the Spirit. But then I assure myself that this is no passing fancy but an impulse that has remained with me, off and on, for over fifty years.

℘℘℘

August 3, 1995

I've not been sleeping well. Either I can't get to sleep or I wake in the small hours of the night and can't get back to sleep. I've considered getting up and praying, but bed is comfortable and my mind is tired. So I stay where I am.

In Morton Kelsey's *Adventure Inward* he recounts a conversation he has with God. It is late at night and Kelsey protests the hour saying that he needs his sleep. God replies that night is the best time to get his full, undivided attention and that it won't hurt Kelsey to do without a little sleep. And so they continue to converse.

Is this what God would have me do? I have always considered sleep to be necessary for my well-being and proper functioning the next day.

I've thought of it as a right and not a gift.

꙳꙳꙳

August 8, 1995

It's 1:30 am and I haven't been asleep, so I'm sitting in the living room writing—I don't know what—in this journal. Does God have something to say to me now that He can't tell me during the day?

There must be concerns of which I'm not aware that keep me awake. Why when I try to listen to some message from God, don't I hear anything?

4 am—With the light of day my misgiving vanished. But I don't think I'll again try to pray in the middle of the night when I'm only half awake.

꙳꙳꙳

August 13, 1995

My erratic sleep pattern is beginning to disturb me. Also, recently, I have experienced pains in my left side, but so far no heart problems have been found.

Last night after a birthday party, I went up on

the roof to walk but quickly became exhausted. I returned to my room, feeling my heart pounding and a shortness of breath. I was in bed at 8:30 and slept until 8:00 this morning. Still tired I fixed a breakfast tray and ate in bed but had no appetite and no desire to get up. I didn't try to go to church but read the Rite 2 Eucharist. Then back to sleep. Now, at 3:30 pm I feel back to normal. I wonder what ails me and think I shall have to consult a doctor.

❦❦❦

August 24, 1995

Last night, while playing bridge with friends, I had a really painful attack of angina which continued for some time. This is something I can no longer ignore. I am grateful to be where I can get nursing care whenever needed. I don't know what would have happened had I been at home alone.

I am confident that I shall get the care that I need as I face having an angioplasty. It may be painful but I have good friends who will pray for me.

My biggest disappointment is that I shall have to cancel plans to go on vacation with my family.

❦❦❦

August 25, 1995

Today I go for a stress test. I have been wearing a pacemaker. Watching the sunrise this morning helped me forget my anxiety and to thank God for such a display of heavenly glory. I am trying to trust Him to strengthen me whatever the verdict.

ᛣᛣᛣ

September 1, 1995

Another "spell" last night, a lesser one this morning. I shall take it easy today. Fortunately my only engagement is to read aloud to my friend Jean.

But I do have many commitments for the next month. Besides preparing for the journaling workshop I have been asked to conduct, I have other important responsibilities as well.

ᛣᛣᛣ

September 8, 1995

By now many people know that I am suffering from angina. Friends call with offers to drive me to the doctor or whatever. I know that I'm being prayed for and that helps.

Two events this week in which I had a leading role went well. I'm grateful for that.

ᛣᛣᛣ

September 14, 1995

Today I go to the hospital for cardiac catheterization.

"Whatever happens, what is, is what I want, only that, but that."

In other words, I shall try to accept the result of this test with equanimity. The surgeon doesn't know what it may reveal. I know in any event I shall rest in God's hands.

ᛣᛣᛣ

September 15, 1995

It's hard to believe that just 26 hours after I entered the hospital I'm back home again. Everything went like clockwork. A balloon device was inserted into one of my coronary arteries to clear it. Afterwards I was told that it had been 90% occluded!

Now I'm ready for bed, very much relieved to have it behind me and looking to the future with renewed strength and energy.

ᛣᛣᛣ

September 30, 1995

Here I am, Lord, at the beginning of a new day. I thank you for a quiet (and as far as I remember, a dreamless) night's sleep. I slept to the music of Hildegarrd of Bingen's "A feather on the breath of God."

This morning's readings included Philippians 4, verse 4: "Rejoice in the Lord always, again I say, rejoice. Let your gentleness be known to everyone. The Lord is near. DO NOT WORRY about anything, but in everything by prayer and supplication with thanksgiving let your requests be known to God. And the peace of God, which surpasses all understanding, will guard your hearts and your minds in Jesus Christ.

Dear God, this is just the advice that I need!

❧❧❧

October 25, 1995

Tonight is another Journaling Workshop. We shall be discussing "Where is God in His world today?" That is one question; a second is, "What can we do to alleviate the sin and suffering that exists? Are we helpless to bring about change?"

I read two newspaper accounts of people who had, by their efforts, made a difference. The first was about a woman minister in an abandoned area of New York City where people lived in abject poverty. She was able to relieve some of their physical needs but she also gave them hope for a brighter future. The second story was about two fathers—one a Jew and one Palestinian—whose sons had been killed. Together they prayed for forgiveness, reconciliation and peace.

Each member of the class was asked to write about some area in their lives where they could make a difference.

November 2, 1995

For three days I have been experiencing pains in my chest—some quite severe. It looks like I may need to have more surgery to open the artery which has again become clogged. This is not a pleasant prospect but having come through it once, I'm sure I shall again.

November 11, 1995

"Humbleness and God-capacity go hand in hand."

Last night I returned home after spending eight

days in the hospital recovering from a stent implant. This time the artery was 98% occluded. The whole process was an ordeal—painful, frightening and uncomfortable.

The morning of the surgery I started to read Ps. 56, the one appointed for today. It began about King David and his enemies and I almost put it down. However, I came to the third verse which read: "When I was afraid, I put my trust in you. In God, whose word I praise, in God I trust. I am not afraid; what can human flesh do to me?"

I felt sure that I could endure anything if I put my whole trust in God. I repeated the words over and over during a long day of waiting. It wasn't until four o'clock that I was taken downstairs and left in a cold cubicle to wait another 40 minutes. That's when I began to shake and have chills, a combination of cold and nerves. Reciting "In God I trust" didn't seem to help much. I simply could not relax and let go.

I spent the next four days having tests—some painful. I know I was a poor patient—fidgety, fussing, and often fuming. I was incapable of prayer but I took comfort that others were praying for me. Where was my "God capacity" when I needed it? I must not assume that being in God's care precludes pain, tedium, and even ill temper. I know that Jesus was "there for me" whether or not I felt his presence.

ᏙᏙᏙ

December 1, 1995

Joy, joy, joy! Getting ready for Christmas should be pure joy. Unfortunately, in our commercial world, it also involves stress and anxiety. What shall I buy for whom and how much should I spend on gifts? I'm trying to minimize these concerns but I don't want to disappoint anyone who might be expecting a present.

The sooner I get my shopping done the sooner my mind will be at peace and I can contemplate that which is the true joy of Christmas.

ᏙᏙᏙ

December 14, 1995

O God, I feel GOOD today! I know I should say 'well' but that doesn't express how I feel. The last stress test showed no sign of the obstruction. The stent is doing its job so far, though I'm told it will take six months to be sure that it is holding.

One reason I've felt well today was an hour-long massage during which I could completely relax physically and mentally. I thought of what Henri Nouwen said about going from active to passive. It involves turning oneself over completely to the care of another person. It requires both humility and trust.

The older one grows the more one must become dependent on other people. It is, I believe, preparation for that final letting go.

A similar idea showed up in another book I am reading: "Jesus wants us for ourselves, not for what we can do for Him."

ᛈᛈᛈ

January 1, 1996

This morning I thought of Mary caring for her week-old infant. I thought how necessary it is for us to tend and nurture the new life which is reborn in us at Christmas. That overflowing sense of love, goodwill, and joy cannot last unless it is cared for. It needs feeding and protection, but it also needs to be made manifest. It is not something we can just hug to ourselves and enjoy.

I perceive this annual Christmas gift from God as being holy and precious, but also a gift to be shared. As the newly born Christ comes into our hearts, we must nurture His growth until the time when He takes full possession of us and we of Him.

My prayers as I begin a New Year are for all the troubled people of the world—for the millions and millions who live in fear, in want, and in despair. God sent His Son to save them all.

ﾉﾟﾉﾟﾉﾟ

January 7, 1996

The storm of the century is upon us! It's been snowing all night and from the looks of things, it will continue to snow all day. Thirty-mile-an-hour gales cause the snow to come down horizontally in very fine dense flakes. A beautiful spectacle as long as I can view it in a warm, cozy room from my 8th floor window.

But I can imagine the discomfort, inconvenience, and suffering it must cause many who lack shelter, for travelers stranded in automobiles without heat, and for those who have the arduous task of keeping the highways open.

I pray for all those unfortunate folk, that their plight may be made less difficult and dangerous by the intervention of others. Obviously, God cannot, or will not intervene directly to provide shelter and rescue motorists, but He does cause others to do so.

I remember many years ago, in a similar storm, Bob and I volunteered to spend the night in a church basement which was a temporary shelter for the homeless. We slept on the chapel floor after seeing that everyone had a bed. It was a rewarding experience.

ᛕᛕᛕ

January 15, 1996

In the "Cloud of Unknowing" the author has this to say regarding contemplative prayer: "God gives us the desire and the will to (pursue) 'You know not what.'" He goes on to say: "Please do not worry if you never know more than this, but go on ever more and more, so that you will keep advancing. In a word, let this thing deal with you and lead you as it will. Let it be active and you passive."

I keep asking myself: why do I have this persistent longing, and to what purpose? Maybe I don't need a purpose aside from believing that it is God who calls and wills me to respond. He will reveal His purpose in His own good time.

ᛕᛕᛕ

January 18, 1996

Today I had a visit from Bill. There are so many questions to which I hoped he could help me find answers.

My first was why it is that some people like himself (and I'm another) feel compelled to dig deeper into the realm of the Spirit, while others are quite content to accept, without questioning, beliefs that have been given to them.

I told him of my "hang-ups," my tendency to question and rationalize and otherwise use my intellect rather than my heart.

For Bill, prayer comes naturally and I don't think he considers why he does what he does—it's what he feels comfortable doing. Often he is rewarded with a sense of God's presence and that is enough.

This doesn't really answer my question, but opens the door to further exploration of where the Spirit is leading me.

ꝕ ꝕ ꝕ

February 21, 1996—Ash Wednesday

A new beginning! The annual observance of Lent offers us a fresh opportunity to follow Jesus as He moved from a ministry of teaching and healing, through suffering and death to ultimate triumph.

I often picture Lent as a long, dark tunnel. When we enter we don't know what kind of tests, temptations, and revelations we may encounter along the way, but we have the assurance that at the end of the tunnel there is light, joy, and new life.

Alan Jones writes in A PASSION FOR PILGRIMAGE concerning Lent: "You are invited into a great drama of transformation, so that together we might be made into something perilous and new." And later, "This is the paradox of transformation—to live is to give away your heart. To love is to give yourself away."

Dear God, as I enter the "tunnel of Lent," may I follow in Jesus' footsteps and allow Him to transform me, that I may give myself more fully to live and love as He did. Amen.

℘℘℘

March 30, 1996

"Only in love can I find you, my God. In love the gates of my soul should spring open, allowing me to breathe new air of freedom and forget my own petty self."—Karl Rahner.

The cross is the perfect symbol for love. The upright represents our self firmly planted in the ground but stretching up to heaven. The crossbar which intersects the upright at the level of the heart is God's love, crossing out our egotistical selves and reaching out to others. In the process we are transformed—the 'gates of our soul spring open' and we find the freedom which Jesus promised when He said "My service is perfect freedom"—freedom from self and freedom to become the self God wants us to be.

Two motions are involved: reaching upward to God and outward towards others. But they are really only one.

卍 卍 卍

April 2, 1996

Each day in Holy Week presents us with an invitation and opportunity to share with Jesus some event or some encounter that made the last week of His life especially poignant.

The week begins with Jesus' dramatic entrance into Jerusalem. Although the crowds hailed Him as Messiah, He knows what lies ahead. He does nothing to avoid the inevitability of His death. Each day He enters the temple and challenges the hypocrisy of

Jewish authority. On the first day He 'cleanses the temple' of those who had made it a marketplace. When He was questioned by Pharisees and Saducees, He responded with wit and wisdom so that they turned away confounded.

During his final days He took time to instruct His disciples and to prepare them for His death, but also promising that He would see them again. Each evening He withdrew to Bethany where He enjoyed the hospitality of his closest friends—Mary, Martha, and Lazarus. The week draws to an end with the observance of the Passover which He shared with His disciples.

Only John tells the story of the footwashing, but under the circumstances and according to custom, it would not have been unusual. It was an example of servanthood which is so in keeping with Jesus' other teachings.

After the supper was over, Jesus and His disciples retreated to the Garden of Gethsemane where, in agony of spirit, He prayed that 'the cup of suffering' might be avoided, but He finally accepted it for what He perceived to be God's will. There was no other way He could have accomplished his mission. Had He escaped (if that were possible) no one would have remembered Him or His teachings. And we, today, would not know Jesus as our Lord and Savior.

ᛒᛒᛒ

April 6, 1996—Good Friday

What were the prayers that Jesus prayed as He hung upon the cross? We only know a few. But I imagine that He must have prayed for His disciples on whom the continuation of His mission would depend once He was gone. He knew their weaknesses—Judas's infidelity, Peter's denial, and their cowardice in not staying with Him during His ordeal. And, of course, He prayed for His mother and His brothers. He prayed, too, I feel sure, for His enemies and all those who hated Him and had conspired against Him. He prayed for their forgiveness and repentance.

Ever sensitive to beauty, Jesus must have grieved over leaving Palestine in the spring-time when all nature gave promise of new life. And surely He prayed for Jerusalem, the city of the prophets, which had turned its back on God. Beyond Jerusalem was His native Galilee and all the places He had taught and ministered. They also must have been in His prayers.

But I don't think His prayers stopped with the places and people He knew. I think they extended to the whole world and all it's inhabitants, the living and the dead, and those yet to be born. And so, I believe He is still praying for us.

❧❧❧

April 15, 1996—Easter Morning

Today we hear the story in John's gospel of Mary Magdalene's encounter with Jesus in the garden. She was the first to go to the tomb and find that the rock had been removed. Without entering, she hurriedly called Peter and John who returned to find the tomb empty. Mary, however, stayed outside and remained after they had left. As she watched and waited a figure approached, whom she mistook for the gardener. It was only when she heard the familiar voice speak her name that she knew it was Jesus. Her only response was "Raboni," Teacher, but meaning so much more. Like Mary, I would like to hear Him call my name.

❧❧❧

May 6, 1996

I am co-leading a class in which we are discussing a book by Marcus Borg entitled MEETING JESUS FOR THE FIRST TIME. Although he challenges a great deal of traditional theology, I find the picture he draws of Jesus, the man, very appealing.

In a chapter called "The Way Less Traveled—The Way That Leads to Life" he asserts that such a way calls for transformation—a total reversal of the world's values, which Borg calls "conventional wisdom." These include the desire for affluence, achievement and adulation. To overcome our desires for what the world deems of value calls for an entirely different set of values—values which were important to Jesus, such as compassion, justice, openness to the Spirit and trust in the grace of God instead of ourselves.

Dear Jesus, I am trying to learn a "new wisdom" from you—how to take a back seat, how to give someone else the credit, how not to look for a reward or even recognition. Lord, it is so hard and goes against my nature. Please help me. Amen.

ᛘᛘᛘ

May 11, 1996

Borg's book has prompted me to review my own beliefs about Jesus. I believe that He lived and died to demonstrate God's love for all people on earth. He hated hypocrisy and small-mindedness. He had the courage to challenge the authority of the Jewish leaders. Through prayer He was in constant communication with God, his Father, whom He addressed with the intimate term "Abba." When His death became inevitable as the price He must pay in order to remain true to what He valued most, He accepted it with courage and in the end, passivity.

Borg's description of Jesus is fourfold. First of all he was a "Spirit Person;" second, He was a teacher of wisdom; third He was a social prophet; and lastly, He was the founder of movement first known as "the Way," later to become the Christian Church. It was only after Easter when Jesus appeared to His disciples in some resurrected form, that the first people accepted Him as the Christ.

All this makes Jesus much more real to me— a person to whom I can relate, rather than an otherworldly figure speaking in pious phrases and a worker of miracles.

It seems to me that the Church would do well to

occasionally reevaluate and reinterpret its beliefs about Jesus in language less doctrinal and based more on experience. I also think it would be a good thing if those of us who profess to be Christians would attempt to put our own faith into our own words.

❧❧❧

May 12, 1996

How do we perceive Jesus today? Do we imagine Him as He looked and dressed 2000 years ago? Or do we picture Him in modern clothes—shirt and tie or maybe jeans? Is it the Christ figure who is the same now as then, or is it the man Jesus as He appeared during His life on earth?

Any sense of Jesus that I have experienced has been in the nature of light, warmth, and a lifting of my spirit.

My friend Bill was here yesterday and I shared these thoughts with him. Although his own concept of Jesus is more objective, he readily accepted my concept. Before leaving he asked if I wished to continue to meet monthly. I replied emphatically, yes. It has been very wonderful to have someone with whom to talk about God and Jesus in unpious (not impious) ways. We can laugh together as well as pray together.

ᛣ ᛣ ᛣ

July 11, 1996

The story of the Good Samaritan is the story about a foreigner who, in his travels, happens on a poor man who has been mercilessly beaten and left to die. At great inconvenience he interrupts his own journey to tend the wounds of this stranger and, at his own expense, he sees that the stranger gets the care he needs. He didn't hesitate to respond immediately no matter the cost to himself.

And so it was with Jesus. He never passed on the other side of the street to avoid a call for help. Often He must have been delayed and often gone without sleep or rest or food to respond when He saw someone in need. I, too often, do my good deeds at my own convenience. I will pay a visit, make a call, write a note, but seldom give up my own agenda to do so.

Dear Lord, help me to be more alert to my neighbor's needs and to respond quickly and cheerfully no matter the inconvenience. I really want to be a 'good neighbor.'

ᛣ ᛣ ᛣ

August 1, 1996

I do not know how to pray as I ought and God is not forcing Himself on me. These past few days have been pleasantly full of activities and I've not felt any compulsion to pray. I must confess I wish God WOULD force Himself on me—take me by the scruff of my neck, put me down and say, "Now pray!" But He doesn't operate that way.

However, the Spirit does help me in my weakness. He/She is ever at work at the core of my being, directing and sustaining me even when I sense nothing.

Perhaps this is what Jesus had in mind when He compared His kingdom with yeast. Once implanted in the dough the yeast quietly and consistently does its work. So, too, the indwelling Spirit is at work in me whether I'm aware of it or not. For this I am grateful.

℘ ℘ ℘

August 19, 1996

This morning I picked out of my bookcase a book which I had first read nearly sixty years ago. It is entitled THE GREAT CONJECTURE: WHO IS THIS JESUS? I thought I might find it outdated, but instead, to my delight, it still has the capacity to bring the person of Jesus vividly alive. In some respects it is not unlike Borg's concept, emphasizing the importance of relationship rather than doctrine. To quote: "People are turning impatiently from the Jesus of dogma to the Jesus of history. It is even true that an eager public is demanding less a Jesus of history than a Jesus of experience."

And further, "We are witnesses of a flaming torch handed down from witness to witness through the centuries and perceiving that the living argument for the living Christ is the living Christian."

And this book, by Winifred Kirkland, was written in 1929!

ᛣᛣᛣ

October 27, 1996

Dear God, at times I'm so befuddled and my vision is beclouded. Please, I pray, disperse the clouds, which obscure the light of your countenance. I want to be able to see clearly what is your will for me. Empty me of all self-desires and fill me with love. I should be much more charitable than I am. Knowing full well my own failings, help me to accept the failings of others. Amen.

It seems that I repeat and repeat the same prayers and yet I change little. Why is this, Lord? Where do I fail in committing myself wholly to you?

I have been reading a book by Alan Jones. One chapter is called "Self-Simplification: The Birth of the Soul." He writes: "Tears flow the moment when we see the contradiction between what we hope for and what we actually are; when we see the deep gulf between the Love that calls us and our response to it." Tears, he says, are a necessary and essential part of our becoming. A sense of dislocation is common to all those who believe and are willing to wait and look. The pain comes when we are caught between the now and the 'not yet' of our identity. How very true!

ƿ ƿ ƿ

December 4, 1996

Thomas Merton emphasizes the need to become our true selves. From birth the pressures of the outer world have shaped us and distorted the unique being which God intended us to be.

It seems to me that old age gives us time and opportunity to look back at our lives and discover where we've gone wrong. In our younger, more active years we don't have time for introspection. Even though I asked God to show me my faults I was unable to perceive them. I felt I was trying my best to live a good and useful life. But I was looking at myself with my own eyes and not with God's. I was being a self in competition with my other selves, judging myself on my achievements. I was satisfied that I was doing as well if not better, than others.

In 1 Thessalonians, chapter 5, Paul writes, "Therefore encourage one another and build one another up." I have been too prone to 'put down' someone so that I might feel superior.

As I approach my 85th birthday, I hope I have a few years left to reverse the order by putting myself down and putting others up.

ΚΩΚΩΚΩ

January 3, 1997

Today I attended an exhibit of the paintings of the French artist De la Tour. He is a master of the use of light and darkness, but this is more than a mere technical device. His paintings have a spiritual quality even though the subjects may be secular.

One that made a special impression on me was a painting of a blind hurdy-gurdy player who seemed to have inner sight. I felt he saw beyond things of this world to things of infinite mystery and beauty. But the picture which most moved me was entitled "The Repentant Peter." Peter is depicted as an old man, his hands clasped tightly in prayer as tears run down his cheeks. On a table at which he sits is a rooster, a reminder of his denial of Jesus, while under the table a candle sheds its light upon Peter's tear-stained face. I also seem to remember that behind Peter's back there was a cross hanging.

Tears, repentance, forgiveness, a light shining in the darkness were all parts of this memorable painting.

❧❧❧

January 8, 1997

"Not infrequently Providence allows us to commit some very palpable fault in order to humiliate us and cause us to take a true measure of ourselves." —author unknown

This happened to me recently when I took it upon myself to criticize a friend. I told her she was opinionated and overbearing with anyone who disagreed with her. Having done so, I was filled with regret and wrote a note apologizing. But the damage was done and our friendship came to an end. This drove home in a painful way how much damage I can do when I express criticism. It's been a humbling experience but has caused me to 'take true measure' of myself and refrain in the future from any form of judgment.

℠℠℠

March 3, 1997

The words of Hymn 140 are those of John Donne. "Wilt Thou forgive that sin, where I begun, which is my sin though it were done before? Wilt thou forgive those sins through which I run, and do run still, though still I do deplore? When thou hadst done, thou hast not done for I have more."

Sins can be forgiven but not forgotten. The remembrance of them is the best insurance against repeating them.

℠℠℠

March 6, 1997

Psalm 42: "As the deer longs for the water-brook, so my soul longs for you, O God. My soul is athirst for you God, athirst for the living God."

When Bill was here last week he asked me how I experienced God. My answer was vague and impersonal—peace, comfort, a joyful presence and, at special times, a radiant light. Seldom as an enveloping, all-consuming fire or as an inexhaustible source of living water.

I thirst to know God in this way. My prayers would be more fervent if I knew that I was addressing them to a living, caring Person—not an abstract Spirit. I have tried in so many ways to conjure up an image of God before offering Him my prayers. But He remains elusive.

ᛏᛏᛏ

March 12, 1997

My mother's birthday. She would be 122. Although she's been dead for 25 years, I think of her often and her love for me is ever-present. It means far more to me today than it did while she was alive. Then I took it for granted, now I am aware of its consistency, patience, and forgiveness. So often it takes a death to open our eyes to the love which was so generously given and so little appreciated at the time.

Is this a fact of life? Does our sin keep us blind to the truth? I don't think I'm wrong to perceive as a universal truth that death has the power to bring about redemption and atonement. Isn't this what took place when Jesus died? People's eyes were opened. They not only saw their beloved in a new light, but became aware of how blind and disloyal they had been. Their lives were transformed, partly, I believe, because they not only saw Jesus for who He was, but they also saw themselves in all their sinfulness. This to me is the true meaning of redemption.

ᛢᛢᛢ

March 14, 1997

One concept I have of God is of a vast ocean in which I, a little fish, have my home. At times I rest on the ocean floor, waiting and gaining strength, nurtured by my environment. At other times I rise to the surface and float, allowing the water to sustain me, letting it take me wherever it will. Then again, I find myself swimming against the current in order to achieve some end of my own.

Dear God, help me always to swim in the current of your love.

ᛢᛢᛢ

April 9, 1997

My friend Jean is near death. It has become a long and painful process. Multiple sclerosis has *paralyzed her from the waist down for years. Now it has reached her throat and she has trouble swallowing. I've just come from spending an hour with her, spooning little chips of ice into her mouth. One might think it was ambrosia from heaven, she was so appreciative. It's heartbreaking to watch her. Even morphine doesn't ease her pain and discomfort.*

I shall spend as much time with her as I can these next few days. She doesn't beg me to stay longer but smiles when I leave and says, "I love you."

ᴪ ᴪ ᴪ

April 11, 1997

Last evening I spent three hours sitting at Jean's bedside. She was restless and uncomfortable and kept repeating "I feel so sick" and crying "help."

How long, O Lord, how long must she suffer like this? There seems no purpose for it. I can do little for her but hope just being there is a comfort. As I sat and prayed I felt You were there, too, sharing her suffering that even You could not relieve. I'm sure you would have if you could.

ᴪ ᴪ ᴪ

April 13, 1997

I've just been informed of Jean's death. I can only rejoice that, at long last, her struggle is over. The timing was good, as her sister had come to be with her.

My prayer for Jean is for peace of mind and spirit now that she is free from the prison of her body. Always gentle, patient, and grateful for small kindnesses, I shall miss her even as I feel relieved that she has left this world.

❧ ❧ ❧

April 15, 1997

A memorial service for Jean was a fitting farewell. Easter hymns were sung and a clergy friend paid tribute to her generous nature, saying, what I feel, that she gave as much as she received. It is a blessing to have known her.

❧ ❧ ❧

April 18, 1997

Bill was here yesterday. He brought me a copy of Henri Nouwen's BEHOLD THE BEAUTY OF THE LORD: PRAYING WITH ICONS. I had seen this book some years ago and despite my effort, it did nothing for me. Now I think I'm ready for it.

The first of the four icons we examined was the Rublev Trinity. Nouwen says you must enter the scene and pray with total attention to what is going on. After gazing intently the icon engraves itself in your mind and can be recalled at any moment. This icon is entitled "The House of Love." It depicts three figures—God the Father, God the Son, and God the Holy Spirit sitting at a table on which there is a chalice. Beneath the table there is a small aperture which represents the narrow gate through which we are invited to enter the House of Love. The gate is small and requires humility and sacrifice of anyone desiring to enter. I know I'm not ready for this but at least I think I better understand the meaning of this icon.

ཀྵཀྵཀྵ

April 23, 1997

This morning I spent some time contemplating Rublev's icon of Jesus. At first it had no appeal for me. The figure is effeminate and the mouth seems too small. But with Nouwen's words to guide me I find a new depth of meaning. He describes Jesus' eyes this way: "They are neither sentimental or judgmental; neither pious or harsh; neither sweet or severe. They are the eyes of God, Who sees us in our most hidden places and loves us with a divine mercy."

Dear Lord, thank You for letting me get a deeper glimpse of who You are.

ΚΟΚΟΚΟ

June 12, 1997

Psalm 70: "Let those who seek You rejoice and be glad in You—but I am poor and needy, hasten to me O God! You are my help and deliverer, O Lord do not delay!"

I had been thinking about being 'poor in spirit' just before reading this verse. At present I feel spiritually impoverished. I'm going through what is often referred to as 'dryness.' I have no inclination to pray, meditate, or read. Recognizing my poverty of spirit helps me to realize my need for God who is "my help and deliverer."

St. Paul also suffered from a sense of weakness and insufficiency when he heard Jesus say to him, "My grace is sufficient for you, for power is made perfect in weakness."

O God, I am in need of your Grace, hasten to help me. O Lord, do not delay!

ᛣᛣᛣ

September 1, 1997

A booklet on aging suggests that before we die we ought to discover ourselves. If I were to try to answer "Who am I?" I would say I am ——— ———, a child of God, married, with children, loving and beloved. But I'm also a sinner, forgiven and repentant, in search of eternal life in God's service. I would continue to describe myself in contradictory terms: I am self-centered, I am generous; I am insecure and I am confident; I am perceptive and I am dull; I am vain and I am humble; I am gregarious and I like to be alone.

But does this really matter as long as God knows who I am? With his help, I am becoming "who He wants me to be." I hope!

ᛣᛣᛣ

September 26, 1997

I am grateful for every manifestation of God in my life—in the many apparent coincidences that occur at unexpected moments; for sunrises and sunsets; for the love of family and friends; for people's appreciation of my endeavors. All these things assure me that God is present at work in my life whether I encounter Him or not. I pray that my faith will remain steadfast even when I perceive no such manifestations. God's presence does not depend on my perceptions. To have experienced grace, no matter how fleeting, is sufficient to sustain me through periods of darkness and doubt.

ᛣ ᛣ ᛣ

September 27, 1997

On Bill's last visit I told him that I thought I had reached the point where I could leave self behind and stop searching inward and look instead upward to God and outward to others. The soul-searching which I have done for so long has been especially intense in recent months. Now it's time to move on.

The soul-searching has been, I think, necessary and fruitful, with the result that I am comfortable with being who I am, accepting my limitations as well as my gifts and offering all to be used by God at His direction.

ᛣ ᛣ ᛣ

October 7, 1997

My sleep is often restless and my mind is filled with thoughts and anxieties about how I shall be able to fill all the commitments I've made for the next six months. So little time left and so much to prepare. I have been asked to again be a co-leader for an 8-week workshop on Marcus Borg's second book THE GOD WE NEVER KNEW. I shall be doing a class on journaling, making a stewardship presentation at my church and writing new resident interviews for the retirement home where I live.

"Lord, temper with tranquility my manifold activity, and may I do my work for thee with very great simplicity. Amen."

❧❧❧

December 6, 1997

I'm beginning a new journal on a blank page. It fits my mood of the moment. I am devoid of thought and unable to pray, I find myself repeating, "please God, please God," but I don't know what it is I'm asking. Hopefully, God knows and will respond. I feel truly 'poor in spirit.' My plea is that I may please God rather than self. But how do I please God? According to Thomas Merton, our desire to please

God is, in itself, pleasing to God. This is a comforting thought.

Dear God, fill my emptiness with your presence, and fill me with the peace and joy of believing that your love upholds and embraces me no matter my mood of the moment. Amen.

ΚΟΚΟΚΟ

January 6, 1998

Epiphany: a time for the miracle of Christmas to become manifest in our lives and in the world. The Wise Men took the news of Jesus' birth back into the world from which they'd come. Christmas must be followed by Epiphany if it is to have any enduring meaning. If not, it remains a sentimental occasion surrounded by tinsel, poinsettia, carols, gifts—nothing that lasts.

What of Christmas remains for me? More joy, more gratitude, more love, I hope. But I want to find ways to share these gifts with others, not just hoard them to my heart.

Dear God, you sent Jesus into our world at Christmastime, may His presence, His love—Your love—remain among us to be manifested in our lives—in my life—to Your glory. Amen.

ΚΟΚΟΚΟ

January 19, 1998

Last night when I couldn't get to sleep, I turned on my back and recited over and over: "Jesus, Son of the living God, have mercy on me." After a while I had the distinct impression that I was being heard. This morning I opened FORWARD DAY BY DAY and found that the Gospel reading was that of Peter's Confession: "You are the Christ, the Son of the Living God."

In the past I have often used the "Jesus prayer" but was not aware that the words were those of St. Peter. Was it more than a coincidence? I have a feeling which I can't explain that sometimes I am on a wavelength that flattens out time. The present is fused with both the past and the future. Peter's words, which I was to read today, were already part of my consciousness last night.

Whatever the explanation, both the prayer and the coincidence are cause of gratitude.

ΚΡΚ

February 9, 1998

In Paul's epistle to the Corinthians, he writes, "By the grace of God I am what I am." This is an example of accepting oneself and all one's limitations. It is really liberating, removing guilt and shame. It brings us peace of mind and actually allows us to be ourselves and enjoy ourselves.

It is natural to feel inadequate to a task but the secret is to leave the outcome to God and not to worry about failure. Peter, having fished all night and caught nothing, was still willing to try again in response to Jesus' command. We often give up too soon. Failure should not discourage us. This applies to prayer as well as fishing or any other endeavor.

Sometimes I pray for what seems a long time and "catch nothing" but if I persist a little longer I am rewarded by a sense of God's presence.

᛫᛫᛫

April 12, 1998—Easter

At 6:30 I was on the roof in time to see the sunrise in the east and a full moon disappear beyond the western horizon. Symbols I discern as the end of a dark night and the beginning of a bright new day. I found myself repeating the words, "He is risen, He is risen, indeed. Alleluia!"

Hope is the Easter message—a sure hope that God is in charge no matter what happens and that He

can and will transform disaster into triumph,
darkness to light, death into life.

ᛪᛪᛪ

May 9, 1998

"Mindful Availability." I've just come across this
phrase in a book that was loaned to me. There is so
much here that I need to hear. I so seldom give my
whole, undivided attention to any one. As the author
writes: "I am of two minds, one that is present and
engaged with what is before me, and another one that
sits on the sidelines and makes comments."

I often do this, even in church. I remark to myself
about the music, I comment on the sermon, I am easily
distracted, even when I pray. The book goes on to
say: "Such deep availability requires a hospitality that
receives people as they are (situations as well), without
necessarily seeking to cure, fix, or repair their
problems. When you practice mindful availability,
you are simply there with your heart open."

I'm always delighted when someone gives me their
complete attention and listens carefully to what I am
saying. I must try to do likewise.

ᛪᛪᛪ

July 20, 1998

Yesterday's gospel was the well-known story of Martha and Mary. Often as I've read it, I've never stopped to wonder what it was that Jesus was telling Mary as she sat at His feet. I would guess that at first they talked about the events of the previous day—the procession which had ushered Jesus into Jerusalem with palm branches and hosannas. Inevitably, I think, this would have led to the question as to why Jesus had come to the city where He knew He had many enemies as well as friends. He knew full well the risk He was taking, but Mary must have kept asking, "Why, oh why must you expose yourself in this way? Why can't you tone down your message so that it will not offend Jewish authority?" So Jesus set about trying to explain that He had to be faithful to the mission with which God had entrusted Him. The message He preached was of God's love for all people. This was far more important than strict adherence to Jewish law. He denounced the Pharisees for their hypocrisy and He broke the law whenever He thought it in conflict with God's way of compassion and justice for all, especially the outcasts, the poor, the sick and the dying.

He wanted Mary to understand that this is what

He had lived for and this is what He must die for. Only through His death could He demonstrate God's all-encompassing love. Only by His willingness to die could He convince at least some of his followers, that salvation was the result of giving oneself for others, rather than a matter of keeping laws. He must have convinced Mary that He had no choice but to accept what awaited Him as God's will.

℘℘℘

August 22, 1998

"Lord, in Thee have I trusted, let me never be put to confusion." These words speak of the conflict between trust and doubt (confusion). "If our trust were but more simple, we could take Him at His word."

My trust is not simple. I'm not always sure what I believe—about God, about Jesus, about His death and resurrection, about my own death. Like the long ago disciples I look for a "sign," some assurance that what I want to believe is believable. The Jews asked Jesus, "What sign are you going to give us that we may see and believe you?" Jesus replied, "The words that I have spoken to you are spirit and life."

I have heard it said that the opposite of faith is not doubt, but certainty. When you have proof that something is true it is no longer a matter of faith. Faith, St. Paul wrote, is the substance of things unseen. We must live our lives trusting that we are being led by God's Spirit, that we have a destination that will be revealed in God's good time. For now we walk in faith.

ᛣᛣᛣ

August 29, 1998

"Solitude is chosen loneliness."

These words appeared in today's FORWARD DAY BY DAY meditation. The word 'chosen' is important here. Lots of people are lonely who do not choose to be so. Chosen loneliness is different, but there is some risk in the choice. At least there is for me. It can be a selfish choice, an avoidance of involvement in other people's lives.

We must learn to choose loneliness for the purpose of deepening our relationships with God and with our neighbor. Sometimes I choose to be alone for selfish reasons. It would be nice if the Holy Spirit would make my priorities clear and direct me when to remain alone and when to seek the company of my fellow residents.

God alone knows when my choice is a matter of

laziness and self-indulgence and when it is for the purpose of spending time in His presence. Lord, help me to perceive the difference.

ᛣᛣᛣ

September 12, 1998

"The pursuit of wholeness (not perfection) must include the imperfect. These imperfections contain all that we have repressed, rejected, denied and disliked about ourselves. When we choose not to obey them as we should, they do not go away entirely. Some of them just go underground." I wish I could remember where I came across these words of wisdom.

The desire for, and the pursuit of, wholeness lies deep within me although I would not have thought to express it in that way. Wholeness, to me, is the same as integration. It is when everything comes together and we are no longer ruled by conflicts. There no longer is a chasm between our faith and our conduct. They become consistent and give to our behavior an authenticity, even when we are wrong and we fail. As the author states, "Wholeness is not perfection." Thank God for that!

ᛣᛣᛣ

October 1998

From the IONA DAYBOOK: "Life has changed me greatly, it has improved me greatly, but it has left me practically the same. I am very critical, egocentric, and vulnerable. I know all my faults so well that I pay them small heed. They are stronger then I am. They are me!"

The truly marvelous part about it is that God still loves me.

ɤ ɤ ɤ

November 11, 1998

Thoughts of confession and repentance have been in my mind and now I find them to be in the subject of today's gospel. I keep on sinning and I keep on repenting and I keep on trusting in God's forgiveness. Recognizing how often I fail keeps me humble and dependant on God's grace.

God, no better than a human parent, can command our obedience. He waits with patience for us to see the light and to turn to Him willingly and to ask His forgiveness. When this happens, there is joy in heaven.

ɤ ɤ ɤ

November 20, 1998

Today's gospel is Luke, chapter 18, which is the story about the judge who cared nothing about the poor widow who came to him seeking justice, but finally, because of her persistence, granted her request.

Earlier in Luke we read of Jesus saying to his disciples "Ask and it will be given you, search and you will find, knock and the door will be opened to you." These are not meant to be just onetime actions but continuing and continuous ones. In our search for God we must keep on knocking at the door whether we get a response or not. It may well be a lifelong pursuit, but we are called upon to persist, as did the widow. It isn't that God withholds himself from us but that He wants to make certain that we really want what we think we want.

Dear Father in heaven, forbid that I should ever stop asking, searching, or knocking. Amen.

ﾞﾞﾞ

January 27, 1999

I recently heard a woman talk about spiritual gifts. In this category she included many things we seldom consider as spiritual—gardening, flower arranging, hospitality, visiting the sick, listening, reading aloud, letter writing. She urged us not to be discouraged by all the pain and the evil in the world, which are beyond reach, but to focus our time and talents in our own backyards, the area where we live.

My experience has been that the more I have used what small gifts I posses, willing to risk failure in the process, the more they have multiplied. It is only by reaching what we consider our limitations that we permit the power of the Holy Spirit to work through us. Over many years, I can see that, trusting God to reinforce my capabilities, I have been increasing in gifts I never suspected I possessed. I am much more confident now of my ability to speak in public, lead prayers, write articles, tutor a child, relate to people. These are not attributes I was born with, they have grown and developed as I have been willing to reach beyond myself, trusting in God's grace.

ᛣᛣᛣ

February 10, 1999

The Lenten issue of FORWARD DAY BY DAY has on its cover a picture of Jesus hanging on the cross, painted by the French artist George Rouault. It depicts a limp figure with eyes closed, utterly exhausted and helpless. "It is finished." He can do no more.

Then, the longer I look I see the eyes open, gazing straight at me. There seems to be something He wants to communicate, a plea that seems to say "I need you, don't leave me, I'm counting on you."

How much of this was in Rouault's mind when he painted his picture? I think he meant to leave it to the beholder to find the message.

ℛℛℛ

February 11, 1999

In Mark, chapter 8, there is a story of Jesus restoring sight to a blind man. It is described this way: "Then Jesus laid hands on his eyes again and he looked intently and his sight was restored and he saw everything clearly."

In a later chapter Mark tells the story of the rich young man who comes to Jesus asking what he must do to inherit eternal life. Before responding, Jesus LOOKS at the young man and loves him.

I like these two stories as they both describe Jesus as LOOKING, really looking, at someone who has come to Him for help. Matthew tells of two blind beggars who accost Jesus. When asked what they wanted they replied: "Lord, let our eyes be opened." Jesus touched their eyes and they regained their sight.

Eyes play an important part in the way we relate to each other. It is necessary to really look at someone if we want to know who they truly are, what they think and what they need.

ﰮﰮﰮ

February 13, 1999

I'm looking again at Rouault's Crucifixion. Again the eyes open and look at me. What is it He wants to tell me? Is this the way He conveys His love for me?

Perhaps He is telling me that I should look more closely at people I meet and see in their eyes their desire to be loved. I don't find this an easy thing to do. I am usually in a hurry and preoccupied by my own thoughts. However, I shall do my best from now on to pay more attention when I speak to people instead of hurrying on about my own business.

ﰮﰮﰮ

February 14, 1999

Today's sermon was about Jesus' Transfiguration when He met with Moses and Elijah. As His disciples watched in terror, a cloud overshadowed them and they heard a voice saying, "This is my Son, the Beloved, listen to Him." Listening is quite as important as looking.

Railroad crossings used to have signs warning drivers as they approached: Stop, Look, and Listen. As a Lenten disciple I shall try to make this a daily practice.

ᏁᏁᏁ

April 1, 1999

Tonight we commemorate Jesus' last meal with His friends. He still had so much to say before leaving them, but it was too late for words. All he could do was to give them an example of His love, hoping that this final act of washing their feet might say more about love and ministry than any amount of teaching. And so it has.

At first His disciples resisted, feeling that they should be the ones washing the feet of their master. How little they understood that love necessitates serving others in humility.

Jesus must have had qualms about His friends' faith and loyalty but, nevertheless, He loved them and prayed that after His death they would remember and understand the import of His action.

Leaving them with so much uncertainty was among the many pains He bore in order to show the extent of His Father's love.

It is truly marvelous that after 2000 years, people remember and reenact the "foot washing" as they celebrate this "Maundy Thursday."

❧ ❧ ❧

April 3, 1999

"He is risen. Alleluia!" I think this ancient Easter greeting should be revived. "Happy Easter" doesn't convey the magnitude of the event that we are celebrating. After all, we wish people "Happy Valentine's Day" and "Happy Birthday" quite glibly. Easter deserves to be different. We are celebrating an extraordinary event. Jesus returned from death and was recognized by his friends. "Alleluia, He is risen!" should be a cry of unfettered joy.

Lent is over. It is finished. Spring is here and so it is only natural that we feel released and renewed. But with all the dreadful happenings in the world—thousands of ethnic Albanians driven from their homes in Kosovo, waiting in cold and rain and snow to be admitted to neighboring countries. This doesn't make for a happy Easter. Jesus' resurrection can fill our hearts with joy but we cannot be really happy as long as there are those who live in fear and pain and despair.

❧ ❧ ❧

April 8, 1999

Today's FORWARD DAY BY DAY begins "Belief is not a construct of the mind; it is not a set of propositions that will be proved or disproved."

I am not meant to live in certainty but in faith with no compulsion to prove what I believe to be true. I want to believe IN the risen Christ, not ABOUT Him.

Thomas, the doubter, exclaimed, "My Lord and My God!" when he encountered the risen Christ. I would like to do the same.

❧ ❧ ❧

April 21, 1999

Psalm 37 begins with the words: "Do not fret" and "Commit your ways to the Lord; trust in Him and He will act."

I do entirely too much "fretting" when things don't go my way. It is a waste of time to fret over things that have happened and can't be changed and won't matter in a month's time or a year's.

The closer I come to the end of my life I realize that my input is not what's important. It is my love and concern for others, kindness, and generosity which will remain when I am gone. I no longer feel I must have my opinions accepted and my accomplishments noticed. This, I find, is a liberating experience. A certain detachment allows me to be more myself and less dependent on anything I do. It helps me find my identity as a person.

ᴋᴘ ᴋᴘ ᴋᴘ

May 5, 1999

Dear God, give me grace to accept cheerfully and meekly those things which hurt and humble me. Help me to keep in mind that you would rather have me loving and kind than popular and successful. The hardest lesson for me to learn is to be submissive, surrendering my desires and opinions in order to achieve peace and harmony.

ᴋᴘ ᴋᴘ ᴋᴘ

May 6, 1999

Must I always live with contradictions? My many selves struggle with each other for supremacy. My fondest desire is to become whole, to be the person

whom God would have me be. But, am I really ready
to surrender all that would entail?

⚜ ⚜ ⚜

May 25, 1999

One day last week I read a meditation about
nomads: "What dignity and 'aristocracy' they have
as they wander from place to place in the desert."
Not only do they have few possessions but they leave
things as they find them. A nomad does not spend his
life as we do, always attempting to change things.
He accepts with cheerfulness and fortitude the
circumstances of his life and so achieves a 'freedom
of soul.'

We can hardly take up a nomadic style of life,
accustomed as we are to our environment, yet we
can learn from the nomad to be content with only
what we have. To use an expression popular in the
60's, we need to learn how to "hang loose," to seek not
to possess but to be possessed.

⚜ ⚜ ⚜

October 10, 1999

Sometimes I have wondered about the purpose of
prayer. I have rather assumed it was to make us

better Christians; that it was meant primarily to equip us for service in the world. Perhaps, it might also give us new insights into what God would have us do and become.

I have just come across a quite different purpose for praying. What it says is that "Jesus wants companions. He wants them for mission, but even more, He wants them for Himself. Jesus' desire for friends is not primarily utilitarian. He does, however, need workers in his vineyard and hopes that some will respond."

Prayer may well result in lives of service, but that is not its main purpose.

᠅ ᠅ ᠅

October 28, 1999

"I give a new commandment, that you love one another. Just as I have loved you, you should love one another. By this everyone will know that you are my disciples, if you have love for one another."

Jesus addresses this command to His closest friends at the last meal that they ate together. It was not a general impersonal, all-inclusive love that He had in mind at that moment, but a specific, personal love, one for another. Despite their differences, their faults and failings, they must continue to love each other in the same way that He has loved them, accepting, encouraging and forgiving each other. They are to be His witnesses by their willingness to follow His example of humble service.

Of the early Church it was said: "See how those Christians love one another."

This command to love and serve others is beautifully expressed in a poem published in FORWARD DAY BY DAY:

> By our love, Lord, by our love,
> Not by creed or propriety,
> Wisdom or style,
> Nor how we seem,
> By our love
> That's all, that's enough,
> That's Christ's own spirit—
> To touch, to care
> To break out of the petty prison
> Of the ego's cell
> To stand up for our sister,
> Cry with our brother,
> Sing with our neighbor
> More love, Lord, more love,
> And the praise be yours. Amen.

ᛣ ᛣ ᛣ

November 6, 1999

A beautiful bright fall day. I'd like to feel that "All's right with the world," but it isn't so. A horrendous cyclone has taken thousands and thousands of lives in India. The survivors are without food and water. The Russians are bombing Chechnya into submission, and in this country there has been two more senseless killings of innocent people.

Will it ever be so, or can we hope for better things in the new century? Dear God, I want to ask, "Where are you?" and "What are you doing to stop so much suffering?" I feel sure you'd intervene if it were in your power to do so, but when you gave mankind free will, you relinquished your own power. The only power you retained is that of love, and it is love alone that can relieve pain and transform evil. I don't suppose you can do anything about natural disasters or you would have done so. Our world is governed by natural laws but there are flaws in its structure that cause earthquakes, cyclones, and hurricanes. Why, I don't know—it is the way that it is and we must accept the consequences and try to alleviate the suffering— suffering which I feel sure, is shared by a loving God. Prompted by his love, brave men and women volunteer as relief workers and go to the aid of victims, often at great risk to themselves. We should be very grateful to them. They are doing our work for us.

All that I can do is to offer my prayers and contribute to relief organizations. I wish there were more.

ᛯᛯᛯ

December 12, 1999—My 88th birthday

I began the day by reciting the opening verses of Psalm 103: "Bless the Lord, O my soul, and all that is within me, bless his holy name. Bless the Lord, O my soul, and forget not all his benefits."

Dear God, for so many years you have guided my life, keeping me pointed in the direction that you want me to go. I have often rebelled, turned aside, been filled with doubt, followed my desires, but always You have called me back. I know that, with Your help, I shall some day come out into the light of Your presence and Your truth. In the meanwhile I wait.

ᛯᛯᛯ

January 1, 2000

Somewhere in the world at this very moment, as I'm writing, people are celebrating the start of a new millennium. In fact they have been doing so for the past twenty-four hours. On television I have been watching Maoris in Australia, Innuits in the frozen region of Canada, Irish, French, Chileans and Parisians, all singing and dancing and celebrating according to their native customs. There is a wonderful spirit of joy, hope and goodwill evident throughout the world.

Whatever ideological and political differences exist among their governments are momentarily submerged and people of many nations unite to welcome the new century. If only this spirit might prevail in the coming year.

ΚΟΚΟΚΟ

January 6, 2000

In a pamphlet entitled "The Path of Waiting," Henri Nouwen deals with two aspects of waiting: our waiting for God and God waiting for us. Much of what he says is familiar territory. Waiting is not wasteful. It becomes meaningful and fruitful when we consider each moment of our lives as belonging to God. We wait in trust and in hope that He will make Himself known to us in the empty places of our lives.

A new concept is that of waiting together, in

community. He writes: "The whole meaning of Christian community lies in offering each other a space in which we wait for what we have already seen." I have considered waiting a personal discipline, something I do alone. But there is a corporate dimension to waiting. The nation waits the outcome of the political impasse we are facing. The world awaits peace, justice and prosperity for all. And Christians await Jesus' final coming in glory.

God on His part must be waiting for us, His children, to forego our selfish, greedy ways and to accept, instead, His priorities of forgiveness, justice, and love.

ᚹᚹᚹ

February 27, 2000

"We become who we are." I have often heard and pondered the meaning of that phrase. It originated with St. Augustine who also wrote "Our hearts are restless till they find rest in Thee." Isn't it true that to 'become who we are' is to find our rest in God? I conceive of God as a magnet drawing us away from our ego-centered selves and ever toward Himself. How much of our 'individuality' do we lose in the process? Should it be that God wants us to lose ourselves entirely in Him, then it must be good!

By means of daily prayer we are challenged, molded, and transformed into the self God would have us be.

꙳꙳꙳

March 23, 2000

In today's gospel Jesus tells His disciples that a lamp belongs on a lampstand, not hidden under a bed. We have each been given a lamp, a light with which to witness to our faith. Lamps may differ in size, shape, and brightness, but when lit they all give out radiance. Our lamp is the mark of God's indwelling Spirit which we must not keep hidden no matter how feeble the light. If we do so it may falter and go out and we may lose it forever.

This story is somewhat like the parable of the talents. The man who was too timid, or lacking in faith, to put his gift to work, lost it. Our talents and our light are sacred trusts that must be put to use. There's a risk involved, but God won't let us down. His power sustains us even when we fail in our endeavors. He puts us back on our feet that we might try again—and again and again.

꙳꙳꙳

March 24, 2000

Today we read the story of Jesus calming the storm. He was asleep in the boat when his friends woke him and wondered how He could be oblivious to the danger they were in.

Was Jesus really asleep or was He "playing possum?" It may have been that He deliberately waited until the situation became desperate before acting. He did act finally, saying to the sea: "Be still." And the storm abated. His disciples were amazed and asked: "Who is this that even the wind obeys him?" Is this not precisely the question Jesus wanted them to ask?

Often in our own lives when we experience fear and anxiety something happens to relax and reassure us. Perhaps Jesus is testing us in the hope that we will ask, as did the disciples: "Who is this?"

ᛣᛣᛣ

March 28, 2000

It's been four years since Bill moved from here and I have missed having someone with whom I can discuss what matters most to me.

Now I think I have found another person with whom I can relate in the same sort of way. She is an experienced spiritual director, which is what I think I want. She will, I feel, guide me to deeper levels of relationship with God. The big question now is: Do I really want to be led in this direction or am I content to remain where I am? I know there is not only spiritual adventure but risk involved. Liz has assured me that God would not call me to places where I would be left alone. His Holy Spirit would always be present to uphold me.

I have heard it said, "Be careful what you wish for, you just might get it." I believe I have. "Dear God, Abba, Father, I thank You for opening a new door for me. Please give me the faith and courage to enter it. If this is what you want of me, please make the road clear." Amen.

ҡҡҡ

April 11, 2000

Today's Washington Post has pictures of starving, neglected and unloved children in Romania, Rwanda, Russia, and other parts of the world. The photos are so grim and the stories so heart-rendering there is a strong temptation to turn away. But should we? These children are precious to God. He loves them and feels for them in their misery. Doesn't He want us to do the same? We can't do anything to alleviate their suffering—and neither can God. If He could, He would. What He does ask is that we commiserate and in so doing our hearts are enlarged.

Dear, loving Father, your love encompasses all who are weak and helpless, show us ways and give us opportunities to reach out, especially to the children, in Jesus' Name and for His sake. Amen.

℣ ℣ ℣

April 28, 2000

The Gospels this week have all been about Jesus appearing to his disciples after he had been put to death on the cross. It was never instant recognition, nor were the appearances at all spectacular. Rather, they occurred during simple acts like taking a walk, fishing, sharing food, hearing a name.

According to John there were many more instances of Jesus appearing to his disciples than he could relate. The book suggests that these appearances continued for a period of forty days.

It was then that He "ascended into heaven," taking

His place at God's right hand. If He had not done so His resurrection would not have been known outside of Galilee, instead of becoming universal. He still appears in unspectacular ways and many times is failed to be recognized.

ΚΡΚΡ

May 5, 2000

The following are all quotations from a book entitled TOO DEEP FOR WORDS by Thelma Hall. "Contemplation will make us not less concerned with the world we live in, but more so." "God is there as He is in all creation and people and events in our ordinary everyday lives." "To see every woman and every man as sister and brother is to participate in the faith vision of the mystic, whose central intuition is the unity of oneness of ALL in God."

The author ends this chapter with a quote from Karl Rahner: "The Christian of the future will be a mystic, or he will not be a Christian at all."

Mysticism is often considered otherworldly and sequestered from the problems which beset our world. What it is actually is the ability to view the world with God's eyes and respond with His love.

ΚΡΚΡ

May 18, 2000

Prayer, I have read, consists of just three words: Yes, Help, Thanks.

"Yes": I accept my gifts and myself. "Help": I want to reach out to others, to accept them without judgment and "Thanks for all that God has done, is doing and will continue to do in my life."

The original "Yes" is the foundation for all else. Without our acquiescence God cannot reach us. But quickly we realize how hard it is to obey and how much we need God's help, which He never withholds when we ask. Thirdly, we realize that we live by the grace of God, without which we can accomplish little of value.

Matthew's Gospel for today (Chapter 5 verse 37) ends with the words: "Yes, yes." I am reminded of the story of Peter in the boat when he heard the Lord calling him to come across the water to Him. Peter, in his usual impulsive way, responds yes to the call but quickly finds himself sinking and cries out for help. When Jesus reaches out and draws him to safety, Peter most assuredly said "thanks" (although the Gospel does not explicitly state this).

This story has often challenged me. Would I get out of the boat knowing the danger of sinking, perhaps even losing my life? I can only pray that Jesus would keep me afloat. As has often happened to me when I stretch beyond my own abilities I find the help and am grateful.

ᚹᚹᚹ

June 10, 2000

"We need humility for our own happiness." Now that's an unusual idea—if we think of humility as self-abasement. But if it frees us from being preoccupied with our needs and ourselves it is indeed, liberating. Humility is not caring whether we are recognized or get credit for what we do. It is the ability to enhance the gifts of others even at our own expense. Humility and humor are closely related insofar as they allow us to laugh at ourselves.

The French have a lovely word, 'debonair,' which describes a cheerful, carefree disposition, one that accepts itself and faces the cares of life with a light heart. This is the way I would like to live.

ᚹᚹᚹ

June 12, 2000

Today's FORWARD DAY BY DAY has humility as it's theme. (I can't seem to get away from the subject.) It quotes from Ephesians: "With all humility and gentleness, with patience, bearing with one another in love." The author of the meditation goes on to say: "True humility is the deep knowledge that God is to be sought and found and served in every person. Humility bows its heart to all, in acknowledgement of the presence of the Holy Spirit there. The gift of humility comes from the heart of Jesus to you."

It is clear that humility cannot be acquired by our own efforts. My concept of humility is transparency when God's Holy Spirit can be seen through us and when we see His spirit in all whom we meet.

⚮⚮⚮

June 21, 2000

Still another thought on the subject of humility. "Access to the kingdom opens to the humble, those who can, at any age be open and ready to receive whatever good gift God has in store."

Jesus said, "unless you change and become like children, you will never enter the Kingdom of Heaven." Those who rely solely on their own power and take pride in their accomplishments have left no room for God in their lives. It is not that God rules them out of His Kingdom, it's that they rule God out. God responds to our weakness and not our strength.

Jesus singled out children because they were vulnerable and helpless, depending wholly on the love of their parents. God is our parent and we are His "dependents."

ᛕᛕᛕ

June 24, 2000

Acts 13:26. "To us the message of salvation has been sent." What is meant by salvation? In the Old Testament it meant to be rescued and saved from some very real enemies. Everytime there was a victory the ancient Jews believed that God had intervened on their behalf and saved them.

The prophet Isaiah, in the 40th chapter of the book named for him, equates salvation with forgiveness. In verse 4 he writes about Judea, "Her warfare is ended and her iniquity pardoned."

In Jesus' day the Jews saw salvation as the result of keeping a multitude of rules and regulations. They also looked for a Messiah to free and save them from Roman domination.

Today, however, questions arise about the

meaning of salvation. John S. Spong in his book, THE CHURCH MUST CHANGE OR DIE, emphatically rejects the concept of Jesus as "Savior" or "rescuer." The question I ask is, 'What does salvation mean to me?' It is not a doctrine I feel I must accept because I have been told "Jesus Christ came into the world to SAVE sinners." Is this the way I think of Him? The answer is 'sort of.' I'm not worried about being 'saved' so I can get into heaven. What I do believe is that through Jesus we see the extent of God's love and forgiveness. This wonderful revelation liberates us from always feeling guilty and unhealthy, it affirms us and gives us confidence to be our better selves. This confidence is what salvation means to me. It is God's great gift.

℘℘℘

June 27, 2000

"O Lord, in thee have I trusted, let me never be confounded."

But confounded I am as a result of some discussions I've been attending based on Bishop Spong's book. I believe there are many ways in which the Church needs to change in order to make its message known and understandable in our modern world of scientific knowledge and biblical scholarship. But in the process of doing so, Spong would eliminate God as both creator of the world and its prime mover.

I don't want to maintain beliefs that run counter to known facts, nor do I want to give up my faith in a God who is "other" than myself, to Whom I can pray and Who guides and sustains my life. I keep searching for a way to reconcile the two. Faith, I think, can lead us into areas where science cannot go. It is based on revelation and on experience, both of which I deem as trustworthy guides.

We have a spirit unexplained in us, which is in communion with the Spirit of God. As St. Paul wrote in Romans, chapter 8, "When we cry 'Abba, father,' it is that very spirit bearing witness that we are children of God."

༄ ༄ ༄

June 28, 2000

For weeks now I have been wrestling with the apparent conflict between a rational, scientific approach to the Gospel message and one that is based on faith. I can no longer live in two worlds; I can no longer sit on the fence with a foot dangling in each.

The challenge to orthodoxy set forth in THE CHURCH

MUST CHANGE OR DIE is, I'm sure, drawing many who have remained skeptics into the Church. And that is good. For my part I am going to turn my back on skepticism and follow the direction in which the Spirit has been leading me.

ᛦᛦᛦ

July 13, 2000

In the IONA DAYBOOK there is a quotation from Dorthea Bloom, a Quaker and an artist. "Revelation comes to us in spite of ourselves. But it seems we are most often open to it when we don't know the answers. It takes courage to trust the unknown mystery itself— out of which revelation comes. Sometimes for me, the Christ figure stands in for mystery, walking on the troubled waters of our world, or the troubled spirit, or leaping from the cross to bless us."

Could the mystery I have often experienced be the hidden presence of Christ? I am drawn to the simplicity of the Quaker faith, unencumbered as it is with doctrine and long formal prayers. "Friends" trust in the mystery and by doing so find Christ at the center of the universe. In a very real way theirs is a mystic religion.

ᛦᛦᛦ

July 16, 2000

Last night on the roof I watched as a full moon appeared and then disappeared behind clouds. First the top half was visible, the lower half hidden from view. Then as the clouds moved upward the lower half emerged while the upper half disappeared from view. Finally as the moon rose higher, above the clouds, it appeared in its fullness like a huge golden ball floating free across the cobalt blue sky.

The hour I spent sometimes walking, sometimes sitting, sometimes praying and sometimes lost in wonder was a revelation of God's glory.

ФФФ

July 17, 2000

My sleep is still troubled by questions I cannot wholly put out of my mind. I still have doubts about the validity of my experiences of God. I keep asking how real are experiences such as the one I had on the roof last night?

Many times in my adult life I have had momentary glimpses of a world beyond—a world of peace, beauty, and a joy in which I became lost.

I call these "little epiphanies." They may be a

product of my imagination, or a response to an intense longing for God, or—and this is what I desperately want to believe—they can be true revelations of God's presence in my life.

ᛜᛜᛜ

August 4, 2000

The marriage at Cana where Jesus turns water into wine was, according to John, the first "sign" that Jesus performed. One wonders why John felt this incident so important that he places it near the beginning of his Gospel. The reason, I believe, is to affirm from the start that Jesus has the power to transform—water into wine being just a metaphor for this power. Water is an ordinary substance, of little value (except where it is scarce) but wine, good wine, enriches, invigorates, and enlivens.

Surely John meant the event to reveal the ability of Jesus to transform our ordinary lives into something new and powerful. The ingredient that makes the miracle possible is the love of Christ. He wants to transform us into His own image.

ᛜᛜᛜ

August 25, 2000

I have been told that Bernard of Clairvaux, a 14th century monk, decribed the spiritual journey as having four stages. First, we start our lives loving ourselves for our own selves. As we grow older we begin to love God for our sake, i.e. for what God can do for us. Thirdly, we come to love God for His own sake, asking nothing for ourselves. The final stage is to learn to love ourselves for God's sake, recognizing that "We dwell in Him, He in us."

I shall spend the next month, more probably the rest of my life, trying to understand and accept a truth which seems to be the opposite of self-denial. The apparent contradiction must come from the fact that we have two selves dwelling together within us. I have an "old self" and a new, true self—the self God wants me to become. As John the Baptist said, in a different context: "The one must decrease so the other can increase."

℘℘℘

August 29, 2000

Richard Foster, in his book SEEKING THE KINGDOM, says "Nothing is more crucial to the heart of God than the transformation of the human personality." It is a very slow process and may take a lifetime. I am reminded of the imperceptible way in which the dripping of water can slowly but surely erode even the hardest of surfaces. This is the way in which God's Holy Spirit works to penetrate the innermost sanctuary of our hearts.

The important factor in the process is continuous daily exposure to God in prayer and meditation. He will do the transforming; our part is to believe it can happen.

℘ ℘ ℘

August 30, 2000

According to Simon Weil (as quoted in the IONA DAYBOOK): "One does not seek God, one waits for God."

All my life I've been a seeker. I'm just now learning to wait.

℘ ℘ ℘

August 31, 2000

"Lord, let me receive the gift of tears." I seldom cry and when I do it is usually the result of frustration, rejection, or self-pity.

Now I find a need to cry but don't know how— I've held back tears for so long. I need to cry when I think of people, even family members, whom I've hurt. I didn't reach out in love when love was needed. I turned away from another's pain when my presence could have been of some comfort. I need to cry in repentance for the grief I've caused.

But also I need to learn to shed tears of compassion. Perhaps the reason I don't is that I don't care deeply enough, or that I want to remain in control. Weeping is to be swept off one's feet and to give in to heartfelt emotion. I doubt that I can make my heart repentant or compassionate, but I can ask God to do so.

‟‟‟

September 5, 2000

This morning just before I was fully awake, I seemed to hear a voice say: "The door is open. Come in and rest in peace."

Did I imagine these words or were they in response to my persistent searching, asking, and knocking? In either case I believe a door has been opened and I have been invited to "rest"—resting, I presume, from so much mental activity.

What of the room to which I've been invited to enter? I picture it as a vacant space, unfurnished and unadorned. Perhaps there's a chair on which I may rest. The resting was an important part of the dream. I'm asked to just be me, leaving outside all my possessions, opinions, and desires. God will supply me with whatever I need and lead me towards whatever goal He has prepared for me.

As I write I know well that such an utter divesting of all I have and all I think I want is quite impossible for me at this time. However, I won't dismiss it, believing "with God all things are possible."

❧❧❧

September 12, 2000

So often on my journey, Providence has supplied me with a book that speaks to me where I am at the moment. It happened again last week. I went to a store to buy a book about which I had heard. I came away with quite another one. As I was browsing, my eye caught sight of David Adam's BORDER LANDS, which is about Celtic spirituality.

The simplicity and openness in which these ancient people expressed their vision of God I find very appealing. They had no organization, no dogma, not even much liturgy, they just worshiped God in everything, every person and every place. Christ was their constant companion. Here is a characteristic prayer:

"Christ, I put my hand in yours, for I am afraid. I bring memories that hurt and a past that pains for your healing and renewal." It continues: "Christ, come enter through the door of the past, into the remembered and the forgotten, into the joys and the sorrows, into the secret room of shame, into the weeping room of sorrow, into the bright room of love. Come, Christ, enter into the conscious and the unconscious, into the roots of my personality. Cleanse me from my secret faults and renew a right spirit within me." Amen.

ᛕᛕᛕ

September 24, 2000

I've read somewhere that there is a difference between conceiving that God dwells in our hearts and that we dwell in His. In the first instance God (in His Spirit) is limited to the size of our heart while if we abide in God's heart there is no limit to the love and power and peace and joy available to us.

Instead of hugging God to ourselves, fitting Him

into the smallness of our hearts, we, dwelling in God's heart, share His love for all His creatures.

I believe the Holy Spirit dwells within each of us, making it possible for us to respond to the external, transcendent heart of God. There is a Celtic prayer which goes "O Lord, I am in Your heart, Your presence enfolds me, Your presence is love."

℘℘℘

October 3, 2000

"Jesus stretched out His hand and touched Him" (Luke 5:13). How important it is to touch one another—love, sympathy, forgiveness, acceptance—so much is communicated by touch.

Some people reach out and touch with a natural ease, others recoil from being touched. I'm not much of a toucher myself. I reserve my hugs and my pats for those dearest to me, family and friends. Jesus touched all sorts of people: lepers, the deaf, the blind, prostitutes and all who came to be healed. His touch did much more than cure physical ills. It was a sacramental conveying of God's loving care and it had the power to heal emotional and spiritual ills as well as bodily ones.

Dear Lord Jesus, give me the gift of touch that I may reach out to the suffering, the lonely and despondent, in your name. Amen.

ᛣᛣᛣ

October 4, 2000

Yesterday I saw the transformation which touching can make in a person. I was sitting and listening to a woman who is always full of woe. She insists on recounting all her ailments. Boring as it was, I tried to listen sympathetically. While she was speaking, another woman came along and, without saying anything, put her arms around her and gave her a hug. No words were spoken but by the expression on her face I could see that it was this physical contact that she needed most.

ᛣᛣᛣ

December 5, 2000

"It is time to see aging as a process of becoming free." This is not how most people feel about aging. Age is confining, it is debilitating, and it makes us dependent on others. Because of physical or mental limitations, we are no longer at liberty to do what we want or go where we want.

This is all too true but there is another aspect to aging we seldom appreciate. We no longer need to strive to achieve, to accomplish, to be popular, to be recognized. We come to know who we are and accept ourselves. In the process of becoming old we find that less and less is important save for our faith in God and His in us.

There is much in our lives that we can do without and so we free ourselves of responsibilities and relinquish the reins, therefore allowing Christ to be the center of our lives.

ΚΡΚ

December 6, 2000

A reading from the IONA DAYBOOK says this: "The more engaged we are in the material world, the more spiritual we become. The more spiritually awake we are, the more generously we will engage in material existence."

Christianity is not an otherworldly religion. The Incarnation is proof enough of God's love for the world. Jesus entered into the pain, and also the pleasures of this world. As far as we can tell, His mode of worship was very simple. He prayed alone, or with His disciples, out in the open in close touch with nature. He also attended synagogue on the Sabbath as was the practice of the Jews. But He taught that the Sabbath was made for man and not vice-versa. I don't think He thought elaborate ritual was important. What was important was the coming of God's Kingdom on earth as in Heaven.

ᚻᚻᚻ

December 13, 2000

A poem by Tagor: "The door is open; oceans and hills all point to the road. The night near your head will stand silent, for death is a call to the Wayfarer."

"The door is open" are the exact words I heard spoken to me two months ago. I did not consider them a call to death, nor do I now. But of course that will be the last call to which we say "yes."

ᚻᚻᚻ

December 27, 2000

Exodus 33:18-23. "Moses wanted to see God's glory but all he was permitted to see was God's back." We would all love to see God in all His glory, but that is beyond the scope of our vision in this life. It may be our reward in the next. In the meantime we can only see God from behind. In retrospect we perceive where

God has been present, although at the time we failed to recognize His Spirit guiding us in the choices we made, in chance encounters, in books that came our way, unsought.

I can look back on my life and see a thread running through it bringing me to the place where I am now, which is exactly the place where I belong. Through doubts and uncertainties, through faults and failures, at critical moments and in everyday occurrences, God "has made his goodness pass before me" and led me to this place.

↣↣↣

December 30, 2000

Beginning a New Year is like stepping over a threshold and entering new territory. Prayer, real communion with God, is also stepping over a threshold and entering a new place. It requires leaving behind our anxieties, our concerns and our desires, or at least handing them over to God. It is seldom a vocal word, nor need it be any kind of revelation. Just a "still, small voice" which may be no voice at all, just an enfolding presence.

When we recross the threshold and return to our mundane lives, we do so with renewed confidence and a light heart. We have left our worries behind with God and we have been assured that whatever difficulties and disappointments the day may bring, we will not have to face them alone.

ᛣᛣᛣ

January 5, 2001

For me, the most meaningful chapter in the Gospels is John 15, and the most meaningful words: "You did not choose me, but I chose you that you might bear fruit."

Once, long ago, I needed to make a difficult decision about undertaking a new enterprise. For, perhaps, the only time in my life, I opened the Bible at random and my eyes rested on these words of Jesus. Ever since, when tempted to abandon my spiritual journey, I realized that I have no choice. God has chosen me, but what fruit He intends me to bear is not clear to me. But that's His business, not mine. My business is to accept each day, abiding in Jesus who is the vine on which my life depends. Apart from Him I can do nothing.

ᛣᛣᛣ

January 14, 2001

"You see, Alison, it's all true, it's all true!" These are the words which I heard God speak to me so many years ago—words that I have kept hidden from others and only sporadically thought about myself. Why have I been so reluctant to make known this extraordinary experience that happened to me? Is it because I fear it may not be believed, or because I fear it might be? It seems the time has come to do so, and leave the consequences to God.

What was it that God was telling me was "all true?"—his existence? His love and need for me? That death is not the end of life, but a new beginning? I believe all these things are true. If life were not eternal so much of our earthly lives would be meaningless. I'm thinking of those who die young with no time to reach fulfillment and of those whose whole lives are limited by poverty or disease.

Eternal life is quality life, life lived in the presence of Christ. It is also a promise of a future life. Since Jesus rose from the dead, so shall we and so shall our loved ones who have preceded us to the grave. They are with God, perhaps a part of God's very being.

I don't think anyone can be sure whether we will continue to be our individual selves or whether God has another plan. It does not matter as long as we believe that "nothing can separate us from the love of God in Christ Jesus."

៛៛៛

January 18, 2001

Today's Gospel (John 21 vs. 18-23) tells of a last conversation between Jesus and Peter. In it Jesus reminds Peter that when he was younger he was able to go wherever he wanted, but when he grew old he would be taken where he did not wish to go. At that moment Peter turns and seeing John, asks: "Lord, what about him?" To which Jesus replies in effect: "That is none of your business. Follow me."

In so many areas of my life I ask, "Why me? What about so and so?" God seems to be leading me in a direction in which I am reluctant to go. He has given me many signs that I am to follow Him, i.e., His Holy Spirit, in some new direction. In a sense, I think a "belt has been fastened around me," taking me where I do not wish to go. I keep asking: "Why, O, Lord, can't I stay comfortably where I am?"

៛៛៛

February 1, 2001

Today's FORWARD DAY BY DAY writer says, "Becoming a Christian leads to joy beyond measure, but let no one think it is a piece of cake."

In Mark's gospel Jesus tells his disciples that "those who want to save their life must lose it." And "those who lose their life for my sake will save it." This is a promise of new and abundant life in Christ, but only if we relinquish much that we hold dear in this earthly life. God doesn't want just a part of us, He wants all of us.

In Alan Jones' book PASSION FOR PILGRIMAGE, he writes, "... being ourselves requires submission." I know this is true. We only become truly free when we turn over our lives to God without reservation and without doubt. This can lead to "joy beyond measure."

℘℘℘

February 21, 2001

St. Paul, in his second letter to the Corinthians writes "When I came to Troas to proclaim the good news of Christ, a door was opened for me ..., but my mind couldn't rest." Paul's mind couldn't rest because he had been unable to find his friend, Titus. Why is it my mind cannot rest even when I believe that "a door has been opened for me?" My search continues—no longer for understanding and faith, but for an immediate, continuous sense of God's presence. I know it's to be had, but I know I must await its coming.

I am reminded of the words of Simon Weil: "We do not search for God, we wait for God."

꒦꒦꒦

February 24, 2001—Shrove Tuesday

Tomorrow Lent begins. I look on Ash Wednesday as one of the most important days in the Church Year. It is the gateway to the forty-day period prior to Easter.

In the service tomorrow we will be reminded of our sinfulness and of the finiteness of our lives. This sounds pretty grim, but really it is an invitation to repentance and reform. Some form of discipline is expedient to strengthen our commitment to Jesus and to enter more deeply into the events of His life. Whatever form of discipline we undertake needs to have a distinct and avowed purpose. We should ask ourselves why we are giving up certain things for Lent—to lose weight, to acquire knowledge, or to strengthen our will power?

These are mostly worthy goals but are not what Lent is all about. They have nothing to do with following Jesus. This is only done with more time set aside for prayers and meditation. By so doing we may be led to some form of abstinence which will free our time and energy to pursue the goal to which God calls us.

For me, Lent is a journey within a journey. It can be a time of adventure and discovery. And, at the end, we have Jesus' promise of new and unending life with Him.

ﾠﾠ ✠✠✠

March 15, 2001

I sleep fitfully, my mind is too busy to rest. Reading over old journals, as I have been doing, is in some ways unsettling. I certainly never intended that my private meditations would ever be made public. Isn't it very presumptuous of me to consider that what I have written will have value for anyone else? And then I ask, how authentic have been the experiences that I have recorded and how sincere have been my prayers and aspirations? How heavily have I borrowed the thoughts of others and how much might I have imagined?

Despite doubts and misgivings, I shall follow what I perceive to be God's will. The fact that I have kept these journals for over twenty years must be assurance that they are for some purpose. It is my hope that they may encourage others to keep a record of their spiritual journeys with Christ and toward Christ. "He is the journey and the journey's end."

Whatever doubts I have about myself, I cannot doubt that it is God who has prompted this endeavor. And so with joy, as well as humility, I entrust them into His hands.

※ ※ ※

March 19, 2001

"For us there is only the trying, the rest is not our business." What this implies is that God welcomes our attempts to comply with His will and that He will take care of the outcome. If we fail, we fail. That is not what is important.

※ ※ ※

April 9, 2001

Yesterday's Palm Sunday liturgy got me thinking about crowds. First, the crowd which accompanied Jesus from Bethany into Jerusalem. It started small—

mostly Jesus' friends who had followed him from Galilee, but it grew as the procession continued on its way. The crowd took up the shouts of Hosanna as many cut palm branches and hailed Jesus as their king.

The second crowd that gathered in Jerusalem was in a different mood. It included, no doubt, some of the same people who followed out of curiosity. It must also have included some of Jesus' followers, but mostly it was made up of ignorant, mindless people who were easily persuaded by the Jewish authorities to take up the cry, "Crucify him!"

Where would I have been in either crowd? In the first instance I probably would have joined in the cheering. It's exciting to find oneself in the midst of a celebration. But I rather think I might have drawn aside, watching and observing from afar. If I had looked hard at the man riding the little donkey I might have noticed how sad He looked. He allowed the crowd to shout Hosanna but I think He knew the acclaim was only momentary and that a quite different reception awaited Him in Jerusalem.

As to that other crowd, which cried, "Crucify him!" where would I have been? Would I have succumbed to the mass hysteria or would I have had the courage to speak out in defense of a man I felt was being unjustly accused—a man whose life had been devoted to healing the sick, denouncing injustice and hypocrisy and proclaiming God's love?

I really do not know for sure where I would have been "when they crucified my Lord." I pray that I would have been at the foot of the cross.

℘℘℘

April 11, 2001

Holy Week is a time to consider crosses and what they signify. Crosses have become fashionable. Movie stars wear them, sports figures wear them, fashion models wear them, and so do many ordinary people. Crosses come in all shapes and sizes. There are large crosses of gold and silver; there are bejeweled crosses and crosses which have been especially designed for the wearer. These crosses receive a great deal of comment and admiration. I sometimes wonder what message people are conveying with the cross they wear.

My own choice is a very simple cross, which I only wear during Lent, and then I keep it hidden. It's more meaningful to me that way. The cross which has the most signifigance for me is the cross of nails from

Coventry Cathedral. These large nails are a reminder of the pain Jesus suffered as they were driven into His hands and feet. This cross also speaks of forgiveness. The words "Father, forgive" are inscribed on the wall behind the altar in the old, burned out cathedral. The people of Coventry are expressing their forgiveness to the Germans who had mercilessly bombed their city.

I cannot look at a cross with indifference. I see it as the supreme symbol of God's love and forgiveness.

ᛣ ᛣ ᛣ

April 13, 2001—Good Friday

To understand the cross one needs to stand under the cross. It is not something one understands with the head but with the heart. It has been said that the crucifixion is not a spectator sport. I cannot stand aside and watch from the distance. Either I need to participate in what's going on, or I should withdraw entirely.

Alan Jones writes in PASSION FOR PILGRIMAGE, "Good Friday is THE day on which I am invited to look into the heart of the mystery of God's passionate love for me."

And I must respond with all the passion of which I am capable. I am not by nature a passionate person. Seldom have I been swept off my feet with deep emotion. As I wrote earlier about being in a crowd—whether a good or evil one—my tendency is to stand aloof and to be an observer rather than a participant. But when it comes to the crucifixion, God does not permit me this option. He either wants me to be totally present, willing to feel His pain, or to withdraw altogether. It is not only physical pain that Jesus suffers as He hangs on the cross, but also pain on behalf of a suffering world.

I asked a friend about ways to observe Good Friday and she suggested going to the Holocaust Museum. This was not what I had expected and I didn't go, but it certainly gave me something to think about. Wherever in the world there is pain, Christ is present. I had read about Christians in North Korea being singled out for the most diabolical torture if they refused to renounce their faith. They were in my prayers as I knelt before the cross.

Alan Jones quotes a poem by Amy Carmichael, in which each verse ends with the words: "Hast thou no scars, hast thou no wounds." I must admit I have very few. My greatest pain comes from the memory of pain

I have inflicted on others, either through indifference or self-love.

How, dear Lord, can I change? Is my heart already too hard to be broken? When I look on Your cross and the pain You endured for love's sake, I know that You are calling me to be compassionate, to cease being an observer and to become more involved wherever there is pain, whether it's my next door neighbor or on the other side of the world.

ᛡᛡᛡ

April 15, 2001—Easter

This morning in a crowded church, I was one of many voices crying out: "He is risen, He is risen indeed!" It was good to be a part of such a crowd and even better to realize that those same shouts were being raised in Churches around the world. God, our God, has triumphed over death and opened the way for all who have faith in Him to share with Him in a new and resurrected life.

The message is for all, but it is also individual. Each one of us will die alone and enter alone into the unknown realms that lies beyond the grave. It would be scary business without Jesus' promise: "I am going ahead to prepare a place for you."

On another long ago Easter I heard the words: "It's all true, it's all true." Death is not an end, but a beginning. A beautiful Celtic prayer—it's really more of an assertion—sums up my conviction that when I die, Christ will be there WAITING for me.

Christ Before Me

"Christ, You have gone before me to prepare a place for me, that where You are I may be also. There is nowhere I can journey that You have not traveled:

"If I went up to heaven, You would be there; if I lay down in the world of the dead, You would be there. If I flew away beyond the East, or lived in the farthest place in the West, You would be there to lead me. You would be there to help me.

"Christ, I do not know what lies ahead, but I do know Who is with me.

"Christ, I do not know where I shall end up, but I do know Who is there before me.

"Christ, the future is not fully unknown to me for You are there before me."

ﷺﷺﷺ